C000220502

WALSALL CORPORATION BUSES

DAVID HARVEY

AMBERLEY

First published 2018

Amberley Publishing
The Hill, Stroud
Gloucestershire, GL5 4EP

www.amberley-books.com

Copyright © David Harvey 2018

The right of David Harvey to be identified as the Author
of this work has been asserted in accordance with the
Copyrights, Designs and Patents Act 1988.

All rights reserved. No part of this book may be reprinted
or reproduced or utilised in any form or by any electronic,
mechanical or other means, now known or hereafter invented,
including photocopying and recording, or in any information
storage or retrieval system, without the permission in writing
from the Publishers.

British Library Cataloguing in Publication Data.
A catalogue record for this book is available from the British Library.

ISBN 978 1 4456 7062 1 (print)
ISBN 978 1 4456 7063 8 (ebook)

Typeset in 10pt on 13pt Sabon.
Typesetting and Origination by Amberley Publishing.
Printed in the UK.

Contents

Introduction

Walsall Corporation began operating tramcars on 1 January 1904, buses in May 1915 and trolleybuses on 22 July 1931. Having jointly operated tram services with the South Staffordshire Tramways Company in the Black Country until 1 October 1930, it became the last operator of trams in the area, on 30 September 1933.

Walsall's Corporation bus fleet at its peak between the late 1950s and the early 1960s numbered around a maximum of 275 or so units and these were always worked extremely hard. The operating area was not just restricted to the town itself but included a huge area that latterly stretched between Birmingham in the south, Wolverhampton in the west, Stafford in the north and Lichfield in the east. Well over half of Walsall's operational mileage was outside the County Borough boundary, and as well as normal routes it ran numerous colliery services in and around the Cannock Chase area, which was still a productive area for coal extraction.

The early motor bus purchases were typical of their time, being used mainly as vehicles to feed the existing tram fleet. Both Mr R. L. Horsfield (1903–1920) and Mr C. Burgess (1920–1926), who left for a new post in Shanghai, slowly expanded the bus fleet, with the last new trams being delivered to the Corporation in 1920. The first motorbus service, between Bloxwich and Hednesford, began on 23 May 1915 using a single-deck Tilling-Stevens TS3 and three more followed later that year, as well as three Daimler single-deckers. By the end of 1920 the motorbus fleet numbered thirty-five vehicles operating on nine further routes in the Cannock Chase Coalfield. These had been taken over from the pioneering services in the Brownhills, Hednesford, Norton Canes and Chasetown, which were operated between October 1912 and 17 April 1915 by the London & North Western Railway, using double-deck Milnes-Daimlers and Commers. All the new Walsall Corporation buses were single-deckers with a B28R layout though these were altered to B32R in January 1921 at the behest of the Board of Trade.

For ease of driving, like any other operators of the period, petrol-electric vehicles were bought, initially from Tilling-Stevens, but by the mid-1920s a number of unique wartime Subsidy Dennis chassis, converted to petrol-electrics by Tilling-Stevens, were being operated. From 1926 Dennis vehicles became the standard motorbus purchase for Walsall, an unusual choice for a West Midlands operator, no doubt helped in 1928 by the Guilford-based company buying all Walsall's time-expired buses in a part-exchange discount to supply new vehicles. From then on until

1941, Dennises were being enthusiastically purchased both as double-deck and single-deck chassis.

The steady abandonments of the tram system led to a resurgence in the purchase of motorbuses. In 1928, both the long Walsall Wood and Birmingham Road tramway routes were abandoned and top-covered, enclosed staircase Dennis H double-deckers were purchased. Under the auspices of William Vane Morland, who was General Manager from 1926 until his departure to Leeds City Transport in 1932, modern Dennis Lance chassis were purchased, although latterly these were augmented by the advanced AEC Regent 661s. On 30 September 1930, the last tram services operated by the South Staffordshire Tramways Company, the dying giant of electric tramway operation in the Black Country, were closed. These ran from Wednesbury to Darlaston, Wednesbury to the Walsall boundary at James Bridge and Darlaston to James Bridge. These were transferred to Walsall Corporation, who took over operation on the following day of what was effectively operated as a circular service until this too was abandoned on 4 April 1931 and converted to motorbus operation with further new double-deckers. This left Walsall Corporation operating its only tram route on the Bloxwich service.

An agreement was reached with Wolverhampton Corporation, who had been operating a single-deck trolleybus service to Willenhall since 16 September 1927, to operate a joint trolleybus service after Walsall had closed down the Walsall–Willenhall tram route on 3 February 1929 and replaced it with a bus service. Mr Morland was reluctant to instigate trolleybus operations but was encouraged to do so by Mr Owen Silvers, the Wolverhampton General Manager, to have through trolleybus running between the two towns. It was decided that the joint trolleybus service should be operated by double-deck vehicles, but through working could not be completed until the road could be lowered underneath the low LNER/MS railway bridge in Horseley Fields. In the whole of his managerial career, this was the only trolleybus route ever built under the aegis of Vane Morland.

The original route to Willenhall was opened on 22 July 1931 and numbered 28. Wolverhampton's shortworkings as far as Willenhall were given the route number 5. The through working of the jointly operated service between Walsall and Wolverhampton began on 16 November 1931, after lowering the carriageway beneath the railway bridge at Horseley Fields was completed. This enabled double-deckers of both Corporations to reach Wolverhampton town centre, though Walsall required only four trolleybuses for the initial service to Willenhall, with the through working by both municipal operators having the route number 29. Two sixty-seat AEC 663Ts and two Guy BTXs were acquired, becoming the only trolleybuses chassis Walsall ever operated by these two manufacturers.

The appointment of Mr M. J. Somerfield as the new General Manager in April 1932 coincided with the increasing need to replace the last Corporation tram route. The second trolleybus service to Bloxwich (route 30) replaced the Corporation's trams. The introduction of trolleybuses on this route was due to the track on the very busy Bloxwich tram route nearing the end of its life; it was not considered economical to renew it despite the last ten open balcony, four-wheel trams, 40–49, having only been built by Brush in 1920 and the preceding batch of UEC-bodied cars numbered 33–39 being just eight years older.

Despite the age and excellent condition of these remaining tramcars, the decision to convert this final tram route in the town was made. As Birchills Depot in Bloxwich Road was already wired up for the Wolverhampton trolleybuses and the depot was located about half way between Walsall town centre and Bloxwich, the added cost of altering the electrical infrastructure must have played an important part in this decision.

An official ceremony was held on Friday 29 September 1933 to inaugurate the new trolleybus service and the last Bloxwich trams ran on 30 September 1933. Normal trolleybus operation began at 10 a.m. on 1 October 1933 using fifteen brand-new Sunbeam MS2 six-wheelers with fleet numbers 155–169. Beadle, Short and Weymann each supplied five bodies as part of this contract. In 1938 another two Sunbeam MS2 six-wheelers were purchased, only this time with Park Royal bodies, while in 1940 another four basically identical vehicles were purchased. Thus by March 1940, the Walsall trolleybus fleet numbered twenty-five vehicles.

Meanwhile, the bus fleet continued to grow rapidly under the General Managership of Mr M. J. Somerfield, with no fewer than twelve Dennis Lance chassis and seventy-eight Dennis Lance IIs and forty-two single-deck Lancet II chassis being purchased between 1931 and 1941, almost to the exclusion of any other manufacturer's products. After 1935 these motorbuses were exclusively bodied by Park Royal. These were bought to expand the operational area of the municipality, but the Dennis chassis were nearly all fitted with too small, underpowered petrol engines.

During the Second World War, with Walsall being in the centre of the Black Country's industrial heartland, seventy-six Guy Arab chassis with a wide variety of MoS-styled coachbuilders' products entered the fleet between 1942 and 1945 in order to provide transport for the many factory workers. During the war, Walsall was offered Daimler CWA6 chassis but managed to always get the robust Guy Arab Is and IIs. It was during this time, on 31 July 1942, when Birchills Garage was hit with incendiaries during a late air raid which destroyed seven buses and damaged other vehicles and caused structural damage to the premises. Many of these wartime buses were rebodied with bodies recycled from the unpopular pre-war Dennis Lance II fleet, while in 1953 ten received new Willowbrook bodies. This extended the lives of the wartime chassis in some cases by over fourteen years.

The wartime fleet was quickly augmented by post-war Guy Arab III 5LW buses with attractively styled Park Royal bodywork. While the chassis of these vehicles were long-lasting and robust, the feeling first felt in the 1930s that bodywork specification was being pared down to a minimum was perpetuated from this point, with bodywork that was bought to the cheapest specification.

In 1951, the last orders placed by Mr Somerfield before his retirement were two batches of further Guy Arab IIIs and Leyland Titan PD2/1s, each being an order for twenty-five buses. They had Park Royal bodies but with idiosyncratic full-fronted bodywork and were the first 27-foot-long buses to enter service. When Ronald Edgley Cox replaced Mr M. J. Somerfield on 1 June 1952, innovative and unusual buses were purchased, usually in 'penny numbers', with the next batch of buses being totally different to the previous order. The result was that from about 1955, the new incumbent's idiosyncratic purchases could be guaranteed to result in a presumed nightmare for the Walsall Corporation engineering staff. The attractive dark and pale blue livery was the first thing to be replaced by Mr Cox, with a dull, all-over bright blue livery with a single thin bright yellow stripe at upper saloon floor level. In later years this gave a shabby and unloved impression, especially as the overworked bus fleet's body maintenance standards fell. Lightweight bodies were purchased on a wide range of chassis, prototypes and demonstrators were bought from about 1955 and a batch of motor buses was considered large if it numbered fifteen. Meanwhile, trolleybus expansion continued apace with new routes and in 1955 the very first two-axle 30-foot double-decker vehicles in the country entered service on the Blakenhall and Bloxwich circular route in the form of twenty-two Sunbeam F4A trolleybuses.

When standardisation finally arrived in 1962, after purchasing a series of 30-foot-long, front-entrance, front-engined buses in the form of Dennis Loline IIs, AEC Regent 2D2RAs and Daimler CVG6/30s, Mr Cox ordered some ninety-nine production short-length Daimler Fleetlines, nearly all with seventy-seat Northern Counties bodies. With the take-over by West Midlands PTE on the near horizon, at the very end of his tenure Mr Cox finally obtained permission to operate his 'dream bus'. Based on a trolleybus design that was stillborn, a thirty-six-foot-long, two-doored, eighty-six-seater double-decker was operated, continuing to the bitter end the diversity and almost perverse lack of standardisation.

1

The Early Bus Fleet

As with many municipal operators, the early buses in Walsall were used as feeder vehicles for the tram routes which operated on the main radial services from the town centre. There were restrictions on expansion during the First World War and single-deckers, initially Tilling-Stevens petrol-electric vehicles and, after 1926, Dennis E types, were operated. These buses began a long association with buses manufactured by the Guildford-based company. The first forays into large-scale double-deck operation began in 1928 with Dennis Hs at the time when the first tramway abandonments took place. In September 1928 the Birmingham Road service was closed, followed by the Willenhall route in February 1929.

1 (DH 901)
DH 901 was originally a single-deck saloon new in August 1913, used by the directors of W. A. Stevens, and was acquired by Walsall Corporation in July 1915; it was probably the vehicle originally registered KT 423. It was offered to Walsall Corporation because Tilling-Stevens was unable to complete the existing order, as it was heavily involved in work for the Ministry of Munitions. A grey-painted double-deck O18/16RO body was fitted before delivery; it was described as a London type body and is seen after it was first repainted in Walsall's fleet livery of dark red and cream. The vehicle kept this second body until late 1919, when it was fitted with a single-deck body. It was re-seated to B32R in January 1921 and was finally withdrawn in April 1928 and sold as a part exchange deal to Dennis Brothers of Guildford along with all of the pre-1920s stock of buses. (D. R. Harvey Collection)

4 (DH 904)

Above: Still fairly new, one of the Tilling-Stevens TS3s built in May 1915, 4 (DH 904), waits in Market Street, Hednesford High Street, about to work on the service back to Walsall by way of Cannock and Great Wyrley. This Dodson B28F-bodied bus was actually the first motorbus to enter service with Walsall. It had petrol-electric transmission, which was considered by the War Department to be too complicated to maintain, resulting in the Tilling-Stevens TS-type chassis not being commandeered for troop transport use in Flanders. Walsall received eight of these buses during the First World War. By being able to purchase Tilling-Stevens chassis, Walsall was able to expand its services into the Cannock Chase area, to the north and north-east of Bloxwich, before any other operator could gain a toe-hold, once the LNWR had given up bus operation with their ancient Milnes-Daimler and Commer double-deckers. (D. R. Harvey Collection)

10 (DH 1082)

Below: One of the five Daimler CCs of March 1916, DH 1082, later given the fleet number 10 in 1921 when it also was reseated to B32R, exhibits its almost tram-like body qualities, which were typical of the period. This body was built by Dodson to a B28R layout and stands prior to delivery, with its dark red and cream livery beautifully lined out. The body has a clerestory roof line which gave both added light and an increase in headroom. It survived in service until January 1928, by which time it had been converted to run on pneumatic tyres. (D. R. Harvey Collection)

7 (DH 1029)

Above: After receiving Royal Assent for the Walsall Corporation Act of 1914, six Daimler Y types were ordered to operate the Corporation's first bus services to Cannock and Hednesford but were impressed by the War Department before they were even delivered. In 1915 Walsall received the first three of the Daimlers that they managed to purchase from the Coventry-based company. The Corporation was fortunate to retain them, as throughout the country similar chassis were usually commandeered by the War Department. Daimler Y-type single-decker 8 (DH 1029) is parked on the access road between High Street and Park Road in Bloxwich. This bus entered service in December 1915 and was fitted with a rear-entrance twenty-seven-seater body built by Willesden-based Christopher Dodson to a design known as the Sheffield type. In 1921 the body was reseated to B32R. It is waiting at the original terminus of the service to Hednesford. Tramcar 34, one of the eight open-balconied, vestibuled tramcars constructed by the United Electric Company in 1912 and mounted on Brill 21E trucks, is about to pass the single-deck bus. The penultimate track alteration on the Bloxwich route took place in the last months of 1920, when the whole of the High Street section from All Saints through the shopping centre and on to the terminus was doubled. The tramcar is leaving the last of the passing loops and enters a single-track section at Park Road, just before the track was doubled. (D. R. Harvey Collection)

20 (DH 1454)

Opposite above: Ah, the joys of starting up a bus on the old starting handle! Or perhaps it was just posed, as the casually positioned cigarette is not quite right for such a strenuous activity. The elder of the gym-slipped schoolgirls looks out of the bus either with interest with a look of 'who is he trying to impress?', or it just might be her dad who is showing off in this mid-1920s view. This lovely period scene shows how basic the buses of the time were, with their matchboard-roofed bodies, tram-like windows and a climb into the saloon that almost, by the standards of today, demanded crampons. This Walsall Corporation bus is 20 (DH 1454), a 1919 Dennis-Stevens petrol-electric that had a Christopher Dodson B28F body boasting electric lighting, solid tyres, life rails one could die for and a lot of fresh air. (D. R. Harvey Collection)

22 (DH 1456)

Below: A normal control early post-First World War bus was 22 (DH 1456). This Tilling-Stevens TS3 entered service in September 1919 and had a Dodson B28R body, again with a clerestory roof. This particular bus was sent on loan as a demonstrator to Birmingham Corporation, though by the time that this occurred, at the end of February 1923, Birmingham was rapidly moving away from petrol-electric transmission. The bus appears to be painted in a pale blue livery, which, although later slightly modified with cream upper works, remained as the standard Walsall livery until about 1936. This bus was sold as part of the 1928 exchange to Dennis Brothers, who promptly converted the single-decker to a showman's vehicle. (D. R. Harvey Collection)

39 (DH 4900)

Above: In 1926 and 1927, Walsall Corporation briefly dabbled in the newly introduced Guy BB chassis. Chassis 39–43 arrived in June and July 1926 and were fitted with Vickers B30D bodywork. These normal control chassis had pneumatic tyres and for the first time had the luxury of front wheel brakes. These neat looking buses only had a four-year life with Walsall, being taken out of service in December 1930. They were designed for one-man operation as the driver, leaning on the offside front wing of his charge, also wears a Bell Punch ticket machine across his uniform. 39 (DH 4900) is well laden as it prepares to leave on its journey to Pelsall from what appears to be St Paul's Street. (D. R. Harvey Collection)

40 (DH 4901)

Below: The Blakenhall Lodge Free Gardeners Annual Juvenile Outing of 1928 seems to be lacking any juveniles as the beribboned gentlemen of the 'the Committee' pose in front of the three hired Walsall Corporation single-deckers. Sexism was alive and well with all the women on the outing being confined to the interior of the buses. The leading bus is an almost new 40 (DH 4901), one of the quintet of Vickers-bodied Guy BBs that entered service in July 1926. The second bus is one of the same batch, numbered 39–43, while the third bus is almost certainly 47 (DH4908), another Vickers-bodied single-decker but this time on a Dennis E forward control chassis. This bus would be rebodied by the West Bromwich-based coachbuilder W. D. Smith in 1934 with a new B32R body. (D. R. Harvey Collection)

44 (DH 4905)

Standing at the exit from Birchills Garage is the very first of Walsall's Dennis Es, 44 (DH 4905), one of fifty-two of this model that entered service with Walsall Corporation Motors between 1926 and 1928. It is about to leave the garage in about 1932 to take up duties on the service to New Invention. These buses became Walsall's standard single-decker between 1926 and 1928. 44 was initially bodied by Vickers to a B32R layout, but was rebodied by the West Bromwich-based coachbuilder W. D. Smith in 1934 and lasted in service until 1944. It is seen here with its original, rather fussily designed old-fashioned body. (R. Marshall Collection)

45 (DH 4906) etc.

Six of the 1926 Vickers-bodied Dennis Es dating from 1926 are professionally posed for posterity when new. These single-deckers were among the first modern buses bought by the Corporation. The identifiable buses from left to right are 45 (DH 4906), 57 (DH 5508), 52 (DH 5503) and 49 (DH 5500). Bus 45 was the only one selected for rebodying by W. D. Smith with a B32R new unit in 1934 and all were withdrawn in 1937, with the exception of 49, which soldiered on until 1944. (D. Seymore Johnson)

48 (DH 4909)

Above: Some twenty-two of the fifty-two Dennis Es built with Vickers B35R bodywork between 1926 and 1928 were rebodied by W. D. Smith of West Bromwich in 1935. The attractive and modern-looking B32R bodies could hardly mask the old-fashioned low-mounted radiator and bonnet line of the Dennis E chassis. 48 (DH 4909), standing at the rear of Birchills Garage, was the last of the five 1934 rebodies, but despite the new body this bus was taken out of service in 1939 and, after a two-year stint as a Walsall Corporation mobile gas showroom, became a National Savings mobile office until 1944, surviving at the back of Birchills Garage until it was eventually broken up in 1958. (D. R. Harvey Collection)

54 (DH 5505)

Below: By about 1941, increased services to aid the war effort brought about a serious driver shortage. Regular drivers were reporting for war service and men unfit for the armed forces were directed to train in the reserved occupation of bus driver. Dennis E 54 (DH 5505) at this time assumed duty as a driver instruction bus; the window behind the driving seat was removed in order to allow the instructor to have access to his pupils. When taking into consideration the skill demanded to drive a Dennis E type, with its lack of self-centering steering, heavy clutch, footbrake and helical gears plus the starting handle being the only means of starting the engine, it must have been quite a task to train a novice driver, but if you could successfully drive 54 you could drive anything! Many did, however, succeed in passing their driving test to become a PSV driver and this included some female drivers. Until after the war, 54 continued to be used for instruction duties and is parked in St Paul's Street railway bridge near to the railway station. The bus was retained in stock until about 1950. (S. N. J. White)

49 (DH 5500)

Above: In 1930, Mr Vane Moreland (then General Manager) authorised the fitting of an experimental Gardner four-cylinder L2 Diesel engine into Dennis E 49 (DH 5500). He was well aware of the economics and power regarding development of the newly developed Diesel oil engine. In order to accommodate the slightly larger engine, the chassis had to be extended some 2 feet, with the radiator protruding forward of the cab front. On 19 September 1930, the bus attended a conference for the Municipal Tramways and Transport Association at Harrogate to demonstrate this new mode of omnibus power. By 1931, Gardners had made substantial progress in Diesel engine design. They had produced a model expressly for transport work and Gardners offered its new 4LW 5.6 litre four-cylinder engine, rated at 68 bhp. 49 ran with its second engine until December 1932, when the new General Manager, Mr M. J. Somerfield, decided it should revert to its Dennis E type petrol engine. The Vickers-bodied bus is working on the Willenhall via Hednesford route with the extended engine compartment required for the long Gardner oil engine. (D. R. Harvey Collection)

59 (DH 5900)

Below: A further pair of thirty-seat normal control Guy BBs entered service in May 1927. The first of the two Vickers B30F-bodied buses was 59 (DH 5900), and it was equipped for one-man operation, though it appears that this specific duty has a driver and a conductor. It was withdrawn in December 1930 and was sold to Burnell's Motors of Weston-super-Mare, who had built up a sizeable fleet of these Guy BBs. (D. R. Harvey Collection)

11 (DH 6300)

Above: The driver of 11 (DH 6300), a 1928 Short H28/24R-bodied Dennis H, strides towards the cab as it stands in front of the Imperial Theatre in Darwell Street in 1932. By this time the bus was already four years old and despite being on pneumatic tyres and having an enclosed driver's cab, rear platform and staircase, looked distinctly old fashioned when compared to other manufacturers' products. The top deck looked almost as if it was placed on a single-deck saloon body, and with a high floor line, the whole structure appeared to be 'perched' on the chassis. The bus had an underpowered side-valve 5.7 litre four-cylinder engine beneath the low-set bonnet and radiator, a cone clutch and a right-hand gate gearchange and a central floor-mounted throttle. Two years later the bus would be extensively rebuilt with a virtually new body, but its mechanical shortcomings ensured that it would only last until October 1938. (D. R. Harvey Collection)

13 (DH 6302)

Opposite above: In their original state, the Dennis Hs fitted with Short H28/24R bodies must have seemed quite modern. They had top-deck covers, enclosed staircases, enclosed drivers' cabs and pneumatic tyres, which in 1928 were not all universal equipment on double-deckers. 13 (DH 6302) had entered service in February 1928 and is seen waiting at the junction in St Paul's Street with Darwell Street when about to leave on the service to Walsall Wood in about 1932. The driver and conductor of the bus pose before starting their journey with DH 6302. The bus might look impressive with its whitewall tyres, but closer inspection reveals the old-fashioned rake of the steering column. The cone clutch and the underpowered, side-valve four-cylinder engine hidden beneath the antiquated low-set bonnet and radiator gave the game away: the Dennis H was very much the last throw of the 1920s-developed double-decker. The three lifeguard rails show the true height of the chassis, while the tram-body style of the lower saloon's opening windows was already becoming dated. Compared to the really trail-blazing chassis being developed by Leyland with their Titan TD1 and AEC with their Regent 661, these buses, for all their 'mod cons', were really last year's models. (D. R. Harvey Collection)

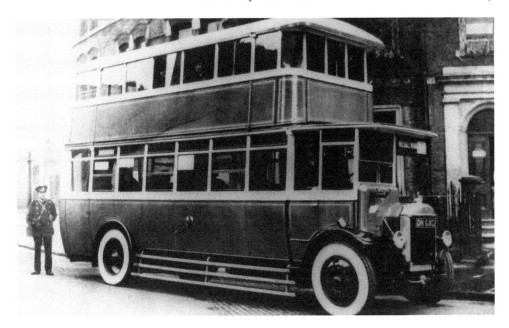

15 (DH6304)

Below: Waiting alongside the impressive cupola-topped premises of the Midland Bank on the corner of St Paul's Street and Bridge Street in about 1935 are two buses that, although looking modern, in fact belong to different generations. The leading bus is 15 (DH 6304), a Dennis H double-decker of 1928 with a right-hand-gate gearchange and the still common centrally placed throttle pedal. The original Short Brothers body was extensively rebuilt in about 1933 with what was effectively a new structure, although apparently using most of the lower deck structure and original fixtures and fittings. The Dennis is working on the 26 route, following the former tram service along Birmingham Road to The Bell Inn. The second bus, 28 (DH 8501), a Brush-bodied 1931 AEC Regent 661, has a much more up-to-date chassis, although still retaining a petrol engine; it is working on the 13 service to Streetly. Behind the AEC bus in Park Street, opposite the entrance to Darwell Street, is a Corporation Dennis E single-decker, while further back up St Paul's Street is the tall nave of St Paul's Church and a lovely Georgian house on the corner of St Paul's Terrace. (W. Bullock)

13 (DH 6302)

Above: Over 2,000 men from Walsall were killed in fighting during the First World War. They are commemorated by the town's Cenotaph, which is located on the site of a bomb that was dropped by Zeppelin *L 21* on 31 January 1916, killing Mrs Slater, the town's Mayoress, and two others who were alighting from totally enclosed tramcar 16. Leading a line-up of seven of the 1928 Dennis Hs in Bradford Place, next to the War Memorial and opposite the south-eastern side of the railway station, is Short-bodied 13 (DH 6302). In original condition, the buses are being used to convey a large number of armed soldiers, which have attracted a big crowd of civilians. As there are no wreaths around the Cenotaph, this was some sort of military parade rather than a Remembrance Day Service. (D. R. Harvey Collection)

19 (DH 6308)

Below: Lined up in Bradford Place, with Walsall's railway station entrance in the distance. The tall brick-built Gothic-styled building dominating the buses is the Science and Art Institute, built in 1888 for use as an adult education establishment. 19 (DH 6308) had been extensively rebuilt in 1934 with an H32/24R seating capacity by the Corporation, with assistance from Gloucester RCW, and is working on the 28 route to Pleck. Behind it is the more modern-looking 43 (DH 8516), a Short-bodied AEC Regent 661 that had entered service in March 1931. It too is working on the circular 38 route but is going 'the other way round' via Darlaston. (D. R. Harvey Collection)

20 (DH 6309)

Above: Parked at the rear of Birchills Garage on 2 March 1938 are four Dennis Hs with heavily rebuilt Short bodies. On the right is 20 (DH 6309), while on the left is 18 (DH 6307). These buses had entered service in 1928 and originally had bodies built with an enclosed driver's cab and an enclosed rear platform and staircase. The eccentrically styled appearance of the bodies quickly became antiquated and as a result the Corporation rebuilt them all between 1933 and 1934. The resulting bodies, based around the original Short Brothers body frames, certainly looked more modern, but alas the Dennis H chassis was, by the mid-1930s, underpowered, unreliable and in its rebuilt form overweight. Within five years of being delivered, the original Short Brothers bodies on all the Dennis Hs would be reconstructed at great expense to make them look cosmetically more modern. Despite the money lavished, or perhaps squandered, on this work only four years earlier, all seventeen of the Dennis Hs went for scrap in 1938, when barely ten years old. (D.R. Harvey Collection)

71 (DH 6402)

Below: Dennis E 71 (DH 6402), dating from April 1928, stands at the top end of Park Street with its posing driver and conductor in Townend Bank when working on the short service from the 'top of the town' to Pleck via Pleck Road. The bus retained its Vickers B31R body until it was taken out of service in 1937. This bus was later rebuilt into a breakdown vehicle in December 1937 and used as such until December 1944. (D. R. Harvey Collection)

74 (DH 6405)

Above: A year after standing in Birchills Garage yard on 25 May 1935, 74 (DH 6405) would be withdrawn from PSV service. Strangely, this Vickers B31R-bodied Dennis E bus had been temporarily converted to a lorry in 1934 along with three others in order to assist in the removal of the abandoned tram infrastructure and then reverted to a bus again for little over a year. 74 is seen in this brief interregnum as the conductor, carrying his box of conducting accoutrements, has a cheery word with his driver before embarking on another duty. (R. Marshall Collection)

90 (DH 6421)

Below: A 1928 Dennis E, 90 (DH 6421), originally with a Vickers B31F body, was converted to a tower wagon in April 1938, in Walsall Corporation's Birchills Depot body shop, and survived in this capacity until February 1960. The rear overhang was cut off and a strong wooden tower erected directly above the rear axle, with a centre screw and winding handle, facilitating a lift of several feet. The front part of the saloon was retained with seats for the breakdown crew, but the rest of the interior was converted for tool chests and spare parts, to cater for overhead problems. It is seen parked on the Townend plot of waste ground in about 1955. The car on the right with a broken nearside headlight is a 1936 Morris Ten. In the background are the distinctive brick chimneys of Dean's Warehouse, which occupied a position at the bottom of Stafford Street. The complicated overhead junction known as Townend was on the corner of Wiseman Street and St Paul's Street. (A. D. Broughall)

91 (DH 6422)

Above: The spotless interior of the newly constructed Birchills Garage is quite striking in this 1928 view over the interior of the garage. Vickers-bodied Dennis Es, including 91 (DH 6422), 75 (DH 6406) and 84 (DH 6415), are all neatly parked. On the right is 38 (DH 47882), the eighteen-seat Guy OND dating from 1926. The body was a 1915 Tilling unit which was fitted to the 1925-built chassis and was instrumental in starting one-man-operated services in the town. It was withdrawn in December 1935. (D. R. Harvey Collection)

93 (DH 6424)

Below: The first joint bus service began on 1 January 1926 when the 14 route to West Bromwich via Fullbrook was begun. Single-decker buses from both Corporations were used, with a half-hourly frequency, until the mid-1930s, when it was converted to double-decker operation. Walsall initially used its only small-sized bus, 38 (DH 4782), a Guy OND, on the new service. The popularity of the new route quickly meant that the larger thirty-two-seater Dennis Es were needed for the busy service. One of the latter, a Vickers-bodied Dennis E, 93 (DH 6424), with a rather old-fashioned-looking Vickers B31R body, stands at the Bradford Place terminus of the West Bromwich service in 1932, at the Bradford Street end of the bus shelters. The ornate wrought-iron bus shelter is impressive, but not exactly storm-proof, as it is open on three sides. The Bradford Street depository was on the corner of Bradford Street. (R. L. Wilson)

21 (DH 7192)

Above: In original as-built condition, the Short Brothers body on Dennis H 21 (DH 7192) looks both modern and antiquated at the same time! The Dennis H was a double-decker produced by the Guildford-based company incorporating modern features but these were tacked onto a chassis design that wasn't quite as radically new as the products coming out of Leyland, Southall and Coventry. These 1928-built Dennis chassis were based on mid-1920s ideas and were little more than a double-decker version of the single-decker E chassis. Within months of entering service, early in the following year, they were found to be underpowered, poor on petrol economy and difficult to drive and to maintain despite their modern body creature comforts. 21 is seen parked at the rear of Birchills Garage when new in May 1929. (D. R. Harvey Collection)

21 (DH 7192)

Opposite above: 21 (DH 72192) in its rebuilt form – only the low-mounted radiator suggests that this Dennis H is anything other than a new bus! The original Short Brothers body had been extensively renovated using parts from Gloucester RC&W that had been assembled by the Corporation's bodybuilders at Birchills Garage. The bus is working on the 2 service from Bloxwich to Willenhall but appears to be parked, albeit with passengers on board, outside Birchills Garage. (D. R. Harvey Collection)

23 (DH 7550)
Below: The original Short bodies fitted to the 23–27 batch Dennis Hs delivered between October and December 1929 were different from the earlier Hs. 23 (DH 7550) is parked on the railway bridge in St Paul's Street. The body style still retained railway carriage-style opening lower saloon windows and a very oddly round styled piano front above the driver's cab. The buses were again rebuilt by the Corporation to the designs of the General Manager using Gloucester RCW components, but they were soon relegated to peak hour duties and were all withdrawn in October 1938. (D. R. Harvey Collection)

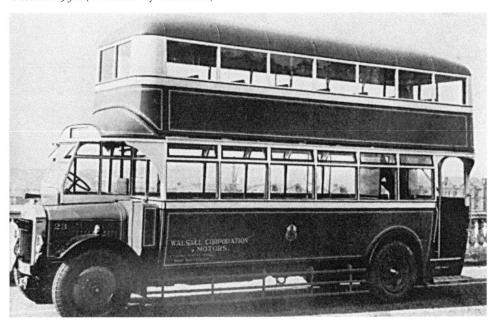

24 (DH 7551)

Standing in St Paul's Street with the nave of St Paul's Church just beyond the Darwell Street junction is 24 (DH 7551), again one of the 23–27 batch with the rounded piano front that incorporated a small destination box. The front upper saloon dome and front windows appear to have been designed 'by a committee' and look quite awful! It is also noticeable that the open single-skinned driver's cab door has no glazing in its upper half. The bus is parked outside the ivy-covered frontage of the Imperial Theatre. This had been built on The Bridge opposite St Paul's Church in Darwell Street as the Agricultural Hall, sponsored by leading local farmers, millers and grain dealers. It could seat up to 1,000 people, and acquired a theatrical licence in 1871, after which operatic and dramatic performances were held. It opened as a permanent theatre on 26 March 1883 but was unprofitable and it was sold in 1885 to become a public hall, known as St George's Hall. It reopened on 22 September 1887 with an increased seating capacity of 1,500 and was used for a time as a music hall. From around 1895 it became known as St George's Theatre. It was rebuilt as the Imperial Theatre, reopening on 22 May 1899 with a seating capacity of 1,600. The new theatre only operated for about a decade before it was also used as a cinema in 1908. It screened its last film in 1968 but survives as a public house with a sympathetically restored interior. (D. R. Harvey Collection)

25 (DH 7552)

A much rebuilt 25 (DH 7552), a Dennis H which had entered service in October 1929, is parked in Bradford Pace in front of the track that led down to the Walsall Canal. It is working on the 38 service to Pleck. The body had been extensively rebuilt in 1935 to a H32/24R layout with a totally modernised front profile to the designs of Mr Somerfield, but the bus behind it suggests that 25 was in its last year of service. Pulled up behind the Dennis H is the former AEC Regent 0661 demonstrator 60 (DHX 504). It had a Park Royal H30/26R body and was acquired by Walsall Corporation in October 1937 when already nineteen months old. The third bus is the 1936 Commercial Motor Show exhibit 189 (ATE 222), a Leyland Titan TD4 with a Leyland H30/26R 'V'-fronted metal-framed body. The large building above the buses is the Science and Art Institute, opened on 24 September 1888 by local MP Sir Charles Forster. A technical day school for fifty-two boy pupils was opened at the institute in 1891. Travelling across Bradford Place is a Morris 14 with wire wheels and a painted radiator shell. (D. R. Harvey Collection)

2

The Early 1930s Bus Fleet

On 17 December 1930, the former South Staffordshire tramway services in the Wednesbury and Darlaston areas were acquired, and along with their own tram service, both were abandoned on 5 March 1931. These conversions meant that some twenty-seven AEC Regents and Dennis Lances were purchased, while the double-decker trolleybus jointly operated service was opened on 16 November 1931 with just four trolleybuses. On 30 September 1933, the last remaining tramway route, to Bloxwich, was abandoned, and replaced by fifteen Sunbeam MS2 trolleybuses.

28 (DH 8501)
Waiting alongside the impressive cupola-topped premises of the Midland Bank on the corner of St Paul's Street and Bridge Street in about 1935 is 28 (DH 8501), the first petrol-engined AEC Regent in the fleet, which had entered service in January 1931, just in time to replace the trams on the routes to Wednesbury, Darlaston and to James Bridge. The bus has a Brush H28/26R body with an exaggerated design of 'V'-shaped upper saloon front windows. It is working on the 12 service to Streetly. (D. R. Harvey Collection)

30 (DH 8503)
The first deliveries of double-deckers that entered service in January 1931 were a pair of AEC Regent 661s and three Dennis Lance Is. These five buses had virtually identical Brush H28/26R bodies with the same extremely angled 'V'-shaped upper saloon front windows. This was done in order to keep down the weight carried by the front axle, but not having a piano-style front. The bus is parked at the Brush Works in Loughborough prior to being delivered to Walsall and looked resplendent in its lined-out light blue and cream relief livery. (Brush)

34 (DH 8507)
Buses 33–37 were also Dennis Lance Is but this time with Beadle H28/24R bodywork. Entering service in February and March 1931, the Beadle bodies had a straight, more modern front profile. 34 (DH 8507) is parked at The Bridge on the stone setts recently vacated by the Bloxwich trams. The bus is working on the 37 circular service to Pleck, Wednesbury and Darlaston, which in 1937 Mr Somerfield unsuccessfully attempted to gain permission to convert to trolleybus operation. Dennis 34 would be withdrawn in December 1944 and sold for scrap. (D. R. Harvey Collection)

37 (DH 8510)

Above: A lady passenger is getting on the bus at the stop outside the Brown Lion Public House in Pleck. The bus is working on the anti-clockwise circular 38 service from Walsall towards Darlaston, which also took in Wednesbury. This route was begun on 5 March 1931 when the Walsall tram service, formerly operated until 17 December 1930 by the South Staffordshire Tramways Company, was abandoned. The bus is 37 (DH 8510) and is a Dennis Lance with an attractively proportioned Beadle H28/24R body. Despite entering service in March 1931, the bus still retains the original style of enclosed rear platform built without the 'turnover' emergency nearside cutaway that was made a legal requirement later the same year under the latest Construction and Use Regulations. (D. R. Harvey Collection)

43 (DH 8516)

Above: Working on the 2 route from Bloxwich to Willenhall, 43 (DH 8516), an AEC Regent 661, helps to clear a large number of waiting passengers when nearly new. This bus entered service in March 1931 as the last member of the six 'normal' Short H26/22R-bodied buses; the last of the batch, numbered 59, was the one with the 'sunshine' opening roof. Within a few years 43 had its seating capacity reduced to H27/23R. The frontal appearance of the upper saloon area on these buses was of a more conventional design than on the recent Brush-bodied buses. 43 remained in service in December 1944 and was sold for spares to the coach operator Noakes of Pensnett during 1945. (D. R. Harvey Collection)

39 (DH 8512)

Opposite below: Inside Birchills Garage, soon after delivery in March 1931, is the complete batch of six AEC Regent 661s with Short H26/22R bodywork. They were numbered 38–43 and the Short bodies featured a long straight staircase, hence the long offside rear panel behind the rear axle. The buses are painted in the new light blue and cream livery that had become standard in 1920 but developed with the post-1931 deliveries when the simplified body styles enhanced this livery. Despite its modern appearance these buses still lacked self-starters and were equipped with a starting handle as well as an outside horn. The nearest bus is 39 (DH 8512), which was taken out of service in December 1944, the whole class being replaced by wartime Guy Arab IIs. (D. R. Harvey Collection)

59 (DH 8517)

59 (DH 8517), in full wartime blackout garb and in the two-tone blue livery, stands in Birchills Garage yard in 1944. This AEC Regent 661 had a Short H28/26R body and entered service in March 1931. Unlike the other six buses with this chassis/body combination, this bus was equipped with a sunshine roof made by Messrs. Wilfrid Overton of Walsall. The Waltman model that was fitted to 59 was an all-weather leather flexible folding central roof section. Tried on six-wheeled LT 405 of London General and a Morecambe Corporation bus, this one was surprisingly long-lived as the bus was not withdrawn until December 1944. The external runners for this folding roof are just visible. (D. R. Harvey Collection)

1 (DH 9041)

Opposite above: Exhibited on the Brush stand at the November 1931 Commercial Motor Show is 1 (DH 9041). This AEC Regent 661 had a layout of H28/26R, which was the largest seating capacity so far supplied on the Regent chassis. This was the last of the fourteen petrol-engined Regent 661 chassis to be ordered despite it being, along with the Dennis Lances, the standard tram replacement bus throughout 1931. On one of the polished wood signs to the front of the bus it states that the body was 'built to the design of W. Vane Moreland Esq., General Manager'. (R. Marshall Collection)

6 (DH 8804)

Opposite below: In June 1931, just before it entered service during the following month, Walsall's 6 (DH 8804), an AEC Regent 661, was selected by Brush, who manufactured the body, to be the subject of the official photograph of the four vehicles numbered 3–6. It is parked in the apparent countryside outside Loughborough but in reality this open land was between the Brush factory and the Great Central Railway line! Surprisingly, even at this date, Walsall specified that the driver's door was to be unglazed. The rest of the design by its coachbuilder was very modern for 1931, save for the eccentric 'V'-shaped upper saloon front windows; this was a ploy to save weight over the front axle, both for the then current legal requirements and to reduce the effort required by the driver to steer the bus. (Brush)

DH 8806

Above: The last four Dennis Lance Is were delivered to Walsall Corporation in July 1931. They were numbered 7–10 and had Brush H28/26R bodies that were the same as the preceding AEC Regent 661s numbered 3–6. In 1930 a replacement called the Lance entered production. This had a 100 bhp, six-cylinder, 6.13 litre overhead valve petrol engine. A fourteen-plate clutch was coupled to a four-speed gearbox. A straight line drive was employed, going to an underslung worm differential on the nearside of the rear axle. The new chassis frame reduced the height by a little over an inch to 23⅜ in. and had a 16 foot 6 inch wheelbase with an overall length of 26 feet for the complete bus. Only forty-one Lance Is were ever built, of which twelve were bought by Walsall Corporation. 8 (DH 8806) has a Brush H28/26R body and is at The Bridge in 1931 while an unidentified open balcony four-wheel tram waits to go to Bloxwich on the service that would be the last to be closed, on 30 September 1933. (R. Wilson)

2 (DH 9042)

Opposite above: Officially posed after also appearing at the 1931 Commercial Motor Show at Olympia is 2 (DH 9042), Walsall's solitary Brush-bodied Dennis Lance II, which seated fifty-four passengers. This was also the last vehicle to be bodied for the undertaking by Brush until 1950. Although it looked much the same as the short-lived previous model, the Lance II chassis was effectively a completely new chassis. Although the earlier Mark II buses had the same radiator as the previous model, the basic components were the same, with the six-cylinder 6.13 litre OHV engine, four-speed gearbox and underslung worm rear axle, but with a new two-plate clutch unit. The chassis frame was completely new, with the side members having a more pronounced downsweep behind the front bulkhead, which was also used as a cross member. Silent bloc shackle bushes and a transmission shock absorber were used to reduce vibrations. The chassis was fitted with a new Dennis-designed worm and nut type, which considerably lightened the steering. (Brush)

101 (DH 9043)

Above: There was a move in the early 1930s to build double-deckers with forward entrances. One of the earliest to be built and subsequently operated by Walsall Corporation was Tilling-Stevens E60A6 DH 9043. Only a handful of this somewhat unsuccessful model were ever constructed. This bus, numbered 101 by Walsall, was shown at the 1931 Commercial Motor Show at Olympia and was equipped with a Beadle H28/25F body built to exhibition standards. This was the new TSM 16 foot 1 inch wheelbase chassis built with a six-cylinder, 6.972 litre conventional petrol engine developing 109 bhp at 2,500 rpm, driving through a four-speed crash gearbox and transmission. The model still retained the central accelerator pedal, which was still being employed on the new Dennis Lance I chassis. The bus is in full Walsall livery and was demonstrated for six months from December 1931 until May 1932. It was eventually sold in May 1932 to John's of Grovesend, near Swansea, who sold out to South Wales Transport in 1938, though it is doubtful if DH 904 was ever operated by them. (T. S. Motors)

The Late 1930s Bus Fleet

From 1934 until the early years of the Second World War the bus fleet grew substantially. At the annual census of vehicles in April 1934, there were ninety-seven motor buses and nineteen trolleybuses in service. Under the regime of the General Manager, M. J. Somerfield, Dennis continued to have a monopoly of the vehicles purchased between 1934 and 1941, with double-decker Lance IIs and Lancet single-deckers being the favoured option, with only two oil-engined demonstrators being purchased in 1936 from other manufacturers. The decision to order petrol-engined vehicles until 1938 would later cause serious operational difficulties, especially with the four-cylindered double-deckers, which were grossly underpowered. For use on lightly trafficked routes from 1934 until 1937, eight Dennis Ace twenty-seat vehicles were purchased. A large central bus station opened in St Paul's Street on 7 August 1935, with new Transport Department offices built adjacent to the bus station. This served bus routes to the north and east of the town, while the earlier Bradford Place Bus Station, adjacent to Walsall's railway station, and in use since 1926, served routes to the south and west. By 1939 there were 157 motor buses and twenty-one trolleybuses in service, with the fleet increasing in size by 53 per cent over the previous five years.

101 (APD 930)

Above: 101 (APD 930), a very early Lance II, was built as a Dennis demonstrator in April 1933. It had a very early Weymann metal-framed H26/24R body and when new it had an Armstrong-Saurer six-cylinder 8.55 litre oil engine. This engine was not a success and so in February 1934, Walsall, ever looking for a bargain, had the bus fitted with a four-cylinder petrol engine and it was used on a free trial for two weeks. It was then acquired on 20 March 1934. It lasted in service until withdrawn in December 1944. (D. R. Harvey Collection)

99 (ADH 972)

Opposite: In July 1934 three Beadle B20F-bodied Dennis Ace buses were purchased. 99 (ADH 972), the middle one of the trio, stands at the exit to Birchills Garage when still quite new in its pale blue livery with a cream-painted waistrail. The Ace was an attractive little bus, ideal for working on lightly trafficked services, and these three were the first of eight buses built for Walsall between 1934 and 137. These three buses were sold to the Belgian Economic Mission for use in that war-ravaged country in 1946, along with the later Park Royal-bodied 107 (CDH 35). (D. R. Harvey Collection)

102 (ADH 934)

102 (ADH 934), a Dennis Lance II with a Weymann H28/24R body, stands in Bradford Place when working on the short circular 3 service to Fullbrook by way of Caldmore Road, Caldmore Green, Milton Street and Palfrey. This service was really only a short working of part of the 14 service, which was jointly operated with West Bromwich Corporation. 102 is still quite new, having entered service in June 1934, although it was exhibited on Dennis's stand at the 1933 Olympia Commercial Motor Show. It originally had an Armstrong-Saurer oil engine and had a seating capacity for fifty-two passengers but prior to acquisition it was reseated to a fifty-seater and fitted with a Dennis four-cylinder 5.7 litre petrol engine. This made buses fitted with this engine grossly underpowered! (D. R. Harvey Collection)

106 (BDH 974)

106 (BDH 974) is seen in St Paul's Bus Station when working to Pelsall. The bus is wearing the late pre-war light and dark blue livery, but still has the full wartime blackout livery and headlight masks. This bus was a Dennis Lance II and had a Gloucester RCW H27/24R body. The bus had entered service in June 1935, but after its original petrol engine had failed both 106 and Park Royal-bodied 111 (CDH 502) were towed to Guildford, and in early 1942 were both fitted with the Dennis O4 four-cylinder 6.8 litre oil engine. As a result of this work, whereas all the rest of these early Dennis Lancet IIs were withdrawn by 1945, both 106 and 111 remained in service until January 1951, with 106 possibly being one of the last Gloucester-bodied buses left operating in the UK. (D. R. Harvey Collection)

108 (CDH 36)

In 1933 Dennis introduced its new twenty-seater model, called the Ace. This had a 3.77 litre four-cylinder petrol engine and was based on the 40 cwt model. To give adequate body space and excellent manoeuvrability, the normal control chassis had the front axle set back so that it was under the rear of the engine, giving the vehicle a 'snout' and earning it the nickname of the 'Flying Pig'. The chromium-plated radiator shell had a rounded top and tapered inwards slightly towards the bottom. In plan view it was slightly 'V'-shaped. It is parked outside the Transport Department's offices in St Paul's Bus Station in March 1955 while being used as a mobile ticket office. (D. F. Parker)

109 (CDH 37)

For many years after it was withdrawn in 1945, Dennis Ace 109 (CDH 37) was driven from Birchills Garage to Bradford Place, where it was parked and used as a mobile canteen for the drivers of buses that terminated in Bradford Place. The Park Royal-bodied bus fulfilled this role in the ancillary fleet until 1961. The back emergency door was used as the entrance with a set of wooden steps in order to gain entrance and a table was fitted on the nearside of the saloon where the tea mugs awaited washing up. The bus was connected to an electric power source, which was used to heat up the tea urn. It must have been an unusual drop for the local milkman who delivered a mixed crate of full cream and stera each day. (A. D. Broughall)

111 (CDH 502)

Above: Parked at the balustraded bridge in St Paul's Street in about 1948 is 111 (CDH 502), a Dennis Lance II with a Park Royal H28/24R body which had entered service in November 1935. Like bus 106 (BDH 974), in early 1942 it was fitted with the Dennis O4 four-cylinder 6.8 litre oil engine and thus prolonged its operational life for another eight years. The bus still retains its 1944 dark and light blue livery. (R. Marshall)

116 (CDH 507)

Opposite below: The short circular 3 service from Bradford Place was only a short working of part of the joint 14 service with West Bromwich Corporation. 116 (CDH 507) is a Dennis with a Park Royal H28/24R body, and entered service in 1935. The bus is parked in Caldmore Green, pronounced 'Calmer'. Although it is a Lance II, it has the much neater, earlier style of radiator that was found on the original Lance I model. Caldmore Green was the centre of a thriving Victorian suburb, which by the mid-1930s could boast its own cinema, The Forum, while opposite was the large Old Kings Arms Public House on the corner of Corporation Street. As well as these, the area could sport a small shopping area and its own Green, although in this winter scene the greenness was somewhat minimal. Standing outside the County Borough of Walsall police box is a policeman in a high-collared tunic, and propped against the box is his regulation bicycle. A Northampton-registered Standard Flying Fourteen is parked at the bus stop while the Morris Isis car behind the bus dates from about 1934. (N. N. Forbes)

60 (DHX 504)

Above: Parked in Walsall Road, Darlaston, just beyond the Bull Stake junction, after the end of hostilities in Europe is 60 (DHX 504). This Park Royal-bodied AEC Regent 0661 had been built in February 1936 as an AEC demonstrator for Walsall. It was the second oil-engined bus in the fleet and was acquired in October 1937. The distinctive Park Royal bodywork was similar to the ones built on the Corporation's own Dennis Lance IIs, though it had the typical Park Royal style of slightly rounded upper saloon front windows coupled with the rounded panel below the windscreen. 60 would remain in service until October 1954. (D. R. Harvey Collection)

189 (ATE 222)

Above: Standing alongside the horse trough in Bradford Place and with the Labour Club in the distant Bradford Street on the corner with Newport Street is Leyland Titan TD4 189 (ATE 222). It was a six-bay construction design known as the 'V-front', and was not very successful, being too lightly framed and suffering from bulkhead failures. A considerable amount of expensive remedial work had to be done by Leyland on vehicles that failed in service, which all but stopped body production at the South Works. A demonstrator, ATE 222, was built with redesigned strengthened bulkheads and exhibited at the October 1935 Commercial Motor Show and was sold to Walsall Corporation in the following February. 189 was acquired from the Leyland Motor Corporation in June 1938 after twelve months' service as a demonstrator in a green and cream livery. After purchase it was quickly repainted from Walsall's two-tone blue. It was originally fitted with a torque converter, but when on trial in Walsall a normal crash box was fitted. During the winter of 1941, 189 was approaching Shelfield from Walsall Wood in icy conditions when it overturned. During the extensive period of body repairs the engine was removed and found to be in need of a complete overhaul, but as it was the only Leyland in Walsall's fleet no spares were in the stores. The engine was taken to a Leyland repair garage situated near Oldbury but it took almost twelve months for 189 to receive its new engine. 189 was withdrawn in January 1956. (D. Williams)

123 (DDH 155)

Opposite below: Parked outside the 1930s-built Ministry of Health Medical Examination Centre building in Hatherton Road is 123 (DDH 155), in about 1948. By now the radiator of the bus had been repainted blue, which spoilt the appearance of 123 even more. This bus was a petrol-engined Dennis Lance II fitted with Dennis's own six-cylinder 6.13 litre OHV engine and which had entered service in August 1936. By this time these petrol engines, although very smoothly balanced, were becoming too underpowered for the heavier bodywork being produced in the mid-1930s and whose fuel consumption performance was barely 4 mpg. The bus was a somewhat spartan version of the standard Park Royal H28/24R bodywork and was one of the first of these buses to be taken out of service, which occurred in September 1949. (S. N. J. White)

128 (DDH 334)

Above: Hatherton Road was used as a parking area for buses waiting to go into Walsall Bus Station. 128 (DDH 334) is standing empty in May 1944 while still in the pre-war streamlined livery augmented by wartime blackout markings and headlamp masks. The bus is carrying an advertisement for Highgate Mild Ales, which was a common adornment on Walsall's buses for many years. The bus has its bonnet side open in order to get more cooling into the engine bay. Behind is 209 (FDH 870), a Dennis Lance II also with a Park Royal H28/24R body, but with the later tall radiator, which necessitated the fitting of a smaller windscreen. (R. A. Mills)

131 (DDH 337)

Above: An almost new Park Royal-bodied Dennis Lance II is about to be rejoined by its driver as it stands in Bradford Place in late 1936. The driver will enter the bus by way of the rear-hinged cab door, a style which was beginning to be phased out. The lined-out light blue and white livery still looks remarkably pristine, though it is rather spoilt by the extensive and detailed advertisement for local coal merchant John Brawn's products, based at the nearby Midland Railway Wharf. (D. R. Harvey Collection)

134 (DDH 801)

Opposite above: The plain all-over pale blue livery as applied to the surviving pre-war Dennis Lancet IIs did the appearance of their Park Royal B38F bodies no favours! Parked in Birchills Garage yard, a slightly battered 134 (DDH 801) awaits its next duty. Somewhat surprisingly, the streamline mouldings have survived a late 1940s body rebuild. When new, these Dennis Lancet IIs were always referred to as 'coaches'! Alongside 134 is 24 (JDH 132), a Guy Arab II 5LW that had received the 1937 Park Royal body formerly mounted on 182 (EDH 310), a 1937-built Dennis Lance II. This rebodying process gave 24 another eleven years of service life. (A. D. Broughall)

171 (DDA 819)

Opposite below: The tall radiator fitted to the new Dennis Lancet II, a model introduced in 1935, suited the single-decker much better than the double-decker equivalent. 171 (DDA 819) is parked in the still unfinished St Paul's Bus Station on 29 March 1937 when barely three months old and has a very attractive Park Royal B38F body painted in the semi-streamlined two-tone blue livery. The bus was new in January 1937 and originally had a Dennis petrol engine. 171 was one of twenty Lancet IIs that were bought with the intention of replacing the unrebodied late 1920s Dennis Es. (J. Cull)

173 (EDH 301)

Above: This splendid view of St Paul's Bus Station dates from within months of its 1938 opening, showing that it was quite big enough for both bus traffic movements and the loading and unloading of passengers. Each of the four platforms was amply signposted for the most myopic of intending travellers and the shelters really did offer waiting folk some measure of protection. In the bus station, on Platform 4 are two Midland Red Metro-Cammell-bodied FEDDs dating from 1936, working on the 118 service to Birmingham. On Platform 3 is Walsall Corporation Dennis Lance II 173 (EDH 301), with a Park Royal body dating from 1937. This bus is working on the 5 route to Brownhills. 173 had a Dennis overhead valve petrol engine and was one of three double-deckers and three Lancet II single-deckers that were out of service due to a lack of spares from 1941 until 1943. Evidently priority for spare parts was eventually granted and these buses returned to service. On the left is 1936 Dennis Lance II 127 (DDH 333), which is about to leave for the Bell Inn on Birmingham Road and is being overtaken by a similar Dennis working on the 13 service to Streetly. At the top of the bus station, in the shadow of the Transport Department Offices, are three more Park Royal-bodied Walsall double-deckers, while on the extreme right, parked outside St Paul's Church, is a Dennis Ace, a model better known by its affection nickname of the 'Flying Pig'. (Walsall Local Studies Library)

184 (EDH 312)

Opposite above: Having worked onto Walsall on the circular 37 Darlaston service, Park Royal H28/24R-bodied Dennis Lance II 184 (EDH 312), the last of the 1937 double-decker order that was delivered in September 1937, is parked awaiting the arrival of its next crew. This bus was the first in the fleet to receive the Dennis o4 oil engine from new. The bus is in the 1944 livery, in which the dark blue lower panels are lacking any of the streamlined paint style. This bus was also the last Lancet II to have the earlier styled radiator, which had been repainted black. 184 would be withdrawn in January 1951 and sold for scrap. (R. A. Mills)

185 (EDH 701)

Below: Standing in Hatherton Road on 29 May 1944 is 185 (EDH 701), the first one of a pair of Park Royal B20F-bodied Dennis Aces delivered in July 1937. These buses had a 3.77 litre four-cylinder engine and were ideal for use on lightly trafficked routes. Both 185 and its twin, 186, lasted in service until July 1957; this was between seven and twelve years longer than the other six Aces bought by the undertaking. It is in full wartime blackout livery and is well marked out in white edging paint. The bus is waiting to go into the bus station before working on the 3 route to Fullbrook. (R. A. Mills)

82 (EDH 860)

Above: The last of the full-sized pre-war single-deckers were Park Royal-bodied Dennis Lancet IIs. A dozen of these buses were delivered in September and October 1937 and although when new they had Dennis four-cylinder petrol engines, they were quickly fitted with the more economical O4 6.8 litre engine. These single-deckers were known as 'coaches' by the Corporation and the shiny, almost new 82 (EDH 860) certainly confirms the reason why they were so-called. It is standing in Hatherton Road and has worked into the town from Cheslyn Hay, Cannock and Norton. (D. R. Harvey Collection)

88 (FDH 704)

Below: Walsall Corporation bought a large number of single-deckers before the Second World War because of the number of operated routes with low bridges. One such route was the service between West Bromwich and Aldridge. On 10 April 1949 Dennis Lancet II 88 (FDH 704), a Park Royal-bodied thirty-eight-seater, stands outside Burton's gentlemen's outfitters in West Bromwich High Street. One of a batch of ten Lancets delivered in 1938, 88 would remain in service until Coronation year. One of the features of High Streets up and down the country about this time was the use of pull-down sun-blinds, which, like women wearing hats, everyone smoking cigarettes and cars backfiring, seems to have faded away into another age. (R. Marshall)

94 (FDH 710)

Above: Parked outside the Transport Department's offices at the top end of St Paul's Bus Station is 94 (FDH 710), a Dennis Lance II with a Park Royal B38F body which entered service as the last member of the ten-strong batch that entered service in July 1938. When new they had the new but unreliable Dennis Lanova four-cylinder 6.5 litre oil engines and these were quickly replaced with the Dennis O4 engine. The bus is wearing the pre-war light and dark blue semi-streamlined livery although it was eventually repainted in the all-over light blue livery. It was withdrawn in 1953 though it was not actually sold until April 1956. (A. D. Broughall)

190 (FDH 851)

Below: Walsall's first four-cylinder oil-engined Lance IIs arrived in September 1938, having the same new frontal structure introduced in 1935 on the Lancet 2. They were fitted with Park Royal H28/26R bodies. 190 (FDH 857) was the first of a batch of twenty-five and when new had a chrome radiator, a single headlight and a chrome-plated starting handle. When withdrawn in September 1951, the body, together with those of twenty-three other Park Royal products, was removed and fitted on a utility Guy chassis. It is parked awaiting its next turn of duty in Hatherton Road in the early post-war years in the two-tone blue livery. (W. J. Haynes)

198 (FDH 859)

Above: The 190–214 class were all fitted with the latest style of the tall radiator, a version of which first appeared in 1935 on the single-deck Lancet II chassis. This also resulted in a very shallow windscreen, which on certain members of the class was made even shorter by the fitting of an externally mounted sun visor. 198 (FDH 859) is parked in St Paul's Street with a pair of railway signals behind the Austin Big Seven and the top of the railway cutting wall. After withdrawal the chassis was scrapped but the body was salvaged, and in 1951 was mounted on 69 (JDH 206), a Guy Arab II 5LW originally with a wartime Massey body, and was withdrawn in February 1961. (S. N. J. White)

199 (FDH 860)

Below: Parked at the top of Park Street, at the top of Townend Bank, in October 1950 is 199 (FDH 860), an oil-engined Dennis Big Four 6.8 litre capacity Dennis Lance II. This bus had a Park Royal H28/26R body and is working on a service to Darlaston Green. It is in the 1944 two-tone blue livery, which painted over the lower streamlined swathe line on the panels. Behind the bus, next to the late Victorian Red Lion Public House, is the Central Piano Saloon, which also sold other musical instruments and sheet music. (D. R. Harvey Collection)

204 (FDH 865)

Above: Advertising the locally brewed Highgate Mild Ales is 1938-built Dennis Lance 204 (FDH 865), fitted with a Park Royal H28/26R body and equipped with the latest Dennis Big Four 04 diesel engine. Twenty-five of these Lance IIs were delivered to Walsall in 1938. The Dennis is standing near The Bull Stake in Walsall Road, Darlaston, near to the large Midland Bank premises. It is 1950, which would be about a year before 204 was withdrawn and its body transferred to a wartime Guy Arab II. The Bull Stake was a favoured lay-over for bus crews, as behind the bus was a café where the crews could top up their billy-cans with tea. (R. Marshall)

206 (FDH 867)

Below: Parked in Bradford Place on 17 April 1939 is 206 (FDH 867). This Dennis Lance II was new in September 1938 and its H28/26R Park Royal body is still painted in its as delivered lined-out livery. It was fitted with a Dennis Big Four 6.8 litre diesel engine. On withdrawal in April 1951 this body was not deemed in a good enough condition to be included in the wartime Guy Arab rebodying scheme and was broken up. It is working on the 38 route to Darlaston and carries an advertisement for *The Birmingham Post*, the broadsheet newspaper which had pretentions towards the professional and businessman end of the journalistic market. (D. R. Harvey Collection)

207 (FDH 868)

Above: Resplendent in the early post-war dark and light blue livery with thin black highlights, 207 (FDH 868) is lying over at the East Cannock Colliery, on East Cannock Road, Hednesford, before taking the outgoing shift of miners back into Walsall. The mine had opened in 1876 and survived to pass to the National Coal Board before closing in 1957. 207, a Park Royal-bodied Dennis Lance II, had entered service in September 1938, but all these Big Four 6.8 litre Diesel-engined double-deckers, especially during the war years and immediately after, struggled with increasing passenger loads, sluggish performance and poor fuel economy. The result was that they were withdrawn as soon as new post-war buses could be delivered, with 207 going in April 1951. But that was not quite it as the Park Royal body was reused on wartime Guy Arab II 38 (JDH 272), lasting in service until July 1961. (D. R. Harvey Collection)

213 (FDH 874)

Below: Parked on the railway bridge in St Paul's Street is Park Royal H28/26R-bodied Dennis Lance II, which was new in October 1938. It is painted in the early post-war light and dark blue livery, which simply painted over the original streamlining mouldings. The bus is carrying an advertisement for the local Highgate Mild Ale, first brewed at the Highgate Brewery in 1898. The brewery was located just to the south of the town centre at the west end of Sandymount Road and was finally closed in 2011. The bus was withdrawn in June 1951, was cut down to waistrail level and survived as a rarely used snowplough in the dark recesses of Birchills Garage. (D. R. Harvey Collection)

215 (HDH 166)

Above: Parked in Walsall's St Paul's Bus Station is the penultimate pre-war Lance II delivered to Walsall Corporation. 215 (HDH 166), built by Dennis Brothers as a demonstration vehicle, was fitted with the latest Dennis O6 Big Six-type 7.58 litre diesel engine. It had a five-speed overdrive gearbox, but this was, perhaps typically of the way in which the Corporation was operated, blanked off! 215 was delivered in November 1939 and received the normal Park Royal body built to Walsall Corporation's usual pared-down specification. The tall, rather ungainly radiator always looked 'wrong', although the semi-streamlined lower dark blue livery band did mask the squashed frontal appearance. The bus is working on the 16 service to Lichfield and is standing at the top end of the bus station on Platform 3 in about 1948. (R. A. Mills)

220 (JPH 828)

Below: The last Dennis Lance II, 220, was also a demonstrator and was registered by Dennis as JPH 828 in Surrey. Built as a normal half-cab, 220 was acquired by Walsall on 17 March 1941 and thus became the last pre-war style bus to enter the fleet. After 1946, this bus was fitted with a full front to its Park Royal body, presumably acting as a trial for the 1951 Guy Arab IIIs and the Leyland Titan PD2/1s. This made 220 look a very different beast, having the ugly Dennis radiator mercifully hidden behind an almost equally hideous, very 'homemade', slatted grill. 220 was the second Lance II bus that had a Dennis O6 Big Six-type 7.58 litre diesel engine, whose development was halted by the Second World War but which was reintroduced in the post-war Lance K3 model. The bus was taken out of service in April 1955 and was scrapped by a Washwood Heath breaker three months later. (R. A. Mills)

4

Wartime Buses

After escaping the worst air raids in the West Midlands area in 1940–41, in the early hours of 31 July 1942, Birchills Garage was hit with incendiary bombs during an air raid. This severely damaged the garage and seven buses were a total loss. Four AEC Regent STs of London Transport and seven Crossley Condors were received on loan from Manchester Corporation Transport as well as six miscellaneous coaches. As a result, and because of all the factories in the town, the Ministry of War Transport authorised the acquisition of new vehicles built to Ministry of Supply specification. Walsall Corporation was offered Daimler CWG5s in 1943, but managed to obtain Guy Arabs throughout the war from 1943 to 1945. A total of seventy-six of these robust buses were subsequently purchased, although subsequent rebodying rather resulted in them being in service far too long for the good of the post-war bus fleet.

192 (HDH 941)
The trees in Bradford Place casting eccentrically shaped shadows on the nearside panels of 192 (HDH 941) can't quite camouflage the shapely pre-war Park Royal bodywork on Walsall's first wartime double-decker. 192 (HDH 941) entered service in November 1942 with a Massey H30/26R body. During 1951 it was rebodied with this 1938 body from a Dennis Lance II, formerly mounted on 201 (FDH 862). In this condition it survived until December 1959. It is parked next to the War Memorial in about 1956 and has been working on a service to Wednesbury. (D. R. Harvey Collection)

195 (HDH 942)

Above: Parked outside the Transport Department's offices in St Paul's Bus Station in about 1945 are two very original-looking wartime buses. The second wartime bus was 195 (HDH 942), which was also a Massey-bodied Guy Arab I with a 7.0 litre Gardner 5LW engine. Unlike its twin, 195 was not rebodied and survived with this original body until November 1955. 195 is in the two-tone blue livery, which somewhat reflects the starkness of Massey Brothers' version of the MoWT outline wartime design. In the distance is 63 (JDH 204), a later Guy Arab II with a slightly softened design of Massey body dating from September 1944 which would be a very early withdrawal in February 1955, almost certainly because many Massey bodies of this part of the war were constructed with badly seasoned wood and any remedial work was considered to be not economically viable. (J. Cull)

ST 1017 (GK 6293)

Below: The destruction of buses at Birchills Garage when it was bombed in July 1942 resulted in a number of buses being sent on loan to Walsall during the following month. Four very elderly former Thomas Tilling petrol-engined AEC Regents were sent on loan, with ST 1017 (GK 6293) being the first to arrive on 14 July 1942. This bus was new in June 1930 and had an H27/25RO body. It was returned to London Transport in September 1944. It is in full wartime garb, even having masked out saloon windows. It is working on the Willenhall route. (D. R. Harvey Collection)

279 (VU3627)

Above: Another nine buses were sent on loan to Walsall Corporation from Manchester in August 1942. These were all Crossley Condors dating from 1930 and 1931. 279 (VU3627) was one of these buses and entered service with a Crossley H28/24R body. It entered service in May 1931, but by the time it arrived in Walsall it had a newer Crossley H30/26R body. The Crossleys were not popular with either the Walsall drivers or garage maintenance staff and 279 was returned to Manchester in January 1943. (MCTD)

179 (HDH 943)

Below: The Ministry of Health Medical Examination Centre occupied a rather utilitarian-looking building in Hatherton Road, outside which Guy Arab I 5LW 179 (HDH 943) is standing. The bus has a utility-styled Park Royal H30/26R body and was built in February 1943, later to be reseated to an increased capacity of H30/29R. This was the first of a total of forty-two Park Royal bodies supplied to Walsall between June 1943 and February 1945. 179 was taken out of service in 1958. Behind the Corporation bus is a Midland Red Brush-bodied SOS FEDD, which has arrived in Walsall from Birmingham. (A. D. Broughall)

205 (HDH 987)

Above: 205 (HDH 987) was quite a rare version of a Guy Arab I. Firstly, it had a Duple H30/26R, which was not a common chassis/body combination. Secondly, it was the only wartime Walsall bus to have the larger 8.4 litre Gardner 6LW engine. The larger engine was usually only allocated to operators in hilly areas as this unit was made available for military vehicles and thus was less readily available for PSVs. The original Guy Arab had short front wings but when fitted with the longer six-cylinder engine required an extended bonnet with the front wings lengthened, with a reverse curve to match the position of the radiator. When the Arab II was introduced this frontal appearance was retained irrespective of whether it had a Gardner 5LW or Gardner 6LW engine, although special Government dispensation had to be given as the chassis was now 7 inches longer than the maximum allowable legal length. 205 is in Hatherton Road in the late 1940s when travelling back into Walsall and is wearing the attractive two-tone blue livery. (R. Marshall)

221 (JDH 33)

Below: 221 was cut down to a single-decker in August 1960, for use on a route requiring a very low-height vehicle, having had the lower saloon extensively rebuilt and a neatly constructed new roof. Despite this expensive rebuild, the service was never introduced and 221 was withdrawn as a PSV in July 1961. Later the same year it was placed into the ancillary fleet and used as a mobile canteen for the benefit of the bus crews whose routes terminated in Bradford Place. 221 was finally withdrawn in April 1968. Even the crate of milk 'at the back door' was renewed daily! (D. Williams)

222 (JDH 34)

Above: The many rebodies on the Guy Arab chassis, caused by the wartime composite bodywork becoming uneconomic to repair, not only saved the Corporation a considerable amount of money but also produced an attractive looking bus. Painted in the 1944 livery, with the lower panels painted dark blue and all the upper areas painted in light blue, 222 (JDH 34) is in Hatherton Road, near to the bus station. The only clue to the bus having a pre-war body is that the cab door is hinged at the rear. This Guy Arab II had originally been built with a MoWT-style Park Royal H30/26R body but this was scrapped and replaced during 1950 with the 1936 Park Royal body from 119 (DDH 151). (R. A. Mills)

13 (JDH 104)

Below: The rebodying of the wartime Guy Arab IIs with pre-war Park Royal bodies in some cases extended the life by over a dozen years. Towards the end of its long career, which ended in November 1962, 13 (JDH 104) passes the Cannock branch of Burton's shop when working on the 1 route in October 1960. The bus has now got the dismal all-over pale blue livery and even the thin yellow lines between the decks appear to be missing. The bus has the 1936 Park Royal body from Dennis Lance II 118 (DDH 150), which had been taken out of service in January 1950. (D. F. Parker)

19 (JDH 110)

Above: Somewhat surprisingly, 19 (JDH 110) was delivered in the streamlined dark blue livery that was introduced in 1937 and was phased out in 1944. The bus is a Park Royal-bodied Guy Arab II and entered service in March 1944. It is loading up with passengers at the bottom passenger stand in St Paul's Bus Station in about 1947. It is carrying an unusual advertisement for the provinces; this was for the monthly *Strand Magazine*, founded by George Newnes, which published short story fiction, including the first serialised Sherlock Holmes detective tales, as well as general interest articles. *The Strand Magazine* was published in the United Kingdom from January 1891 until March 1950, by which time it had been reduced to digest size. 19 received a new Willowbrook H30/26R body which was built to the unusual width of 7 feet 9 inches and their tall, gaunt appearance necessitated their height subsequently being lowered by altering the springing. 19 re-entered service in October 1953, renumbered 207, and was withdrawn in April 1968. (D. R. Harvey Collection)

24 (JDH 132)

*Below:*In June 1944 24 (JDH 132) was delivered to Walsall Corporation. It arrived in an all-over grey livery and entered service in this colour. It is working on the Bloxwich service and is awaiting a new batch of passengers in St Paul's Bus Station when new. This Guy Arab II had a Strachan H30/26R body, but these bodies were noted for their general lack of longevity. It was rebodied in June 1951 with a 1937 Park Royal body from Dennis Lance II 182 (EDH 310) and lasted until February 1962 before becoming a driver trainer for the next fourteen months. (D. R. Harvey Collection)

44 (JDH 136)

Above: About twenty years after the tramcars were withdrawn, Guy Arab II 44 (JDH 136) stands in Walsall Road at The Bull Stake junction in Darlaston. The Gardner 5LW-powered bus entered service in June 1944 and was fitted with a MoWT utility Park Royal H30/26R body. By 1950 the bus had been equipped with upholstered seats, replacing the original wooden-slatted ones, but still only has a pair of opening side windows in each saloon. It was withdrawn in December 1955. 44 is standing outside George Foden's Gents Hairdressers, which, as well as selling Brylcream hair cream, also seems to sell cigarettes, including the cough-inducing Turf brand as well as other more unmentionable 'gentlemen's weekend requisites'. The headscarfed woman on the extreme left is coming out of King Street, which led to the main shopping area of the town and Darlaston's Town Hall, built in 1888 to commemorate Victoria's Golden Jubilee. (R. Marshall)

65 (JDH 195)

Below: The conductor stands on the front step next to the radiator in order to reach for the canopy-mounted destination blind-winding handle. 65 (JDH 195), a Strachan-bodied Guy Arab II, stands in the bus station, in the shadow of St Paul's Church, when freshly repainted in the all-over light blue livery. These Acton-built bodies could be easily identified by the three windows in the driver's cab door as well as by having a very straight and tall-looking rear profile. Despite the general fragility of Strachan wartime bodywork, 65 was the exception that proved the rule as it was withdrawn in April 1963, having been renumbered 165 just a month earlier. (A. D. Broughall)

50 (JDH 199)

Above: The rebodying of the wartime Guy Arab IIs with pre-war Park Royal bodywork taken from Dennis Lance IIs produced a variety of different styles of cab apron and windscreen depths. For example, 50 (JDH 199), parked in Birchills Garage yard soon after being rebodied, has a bulbous cab apron and a small, short windscreen. It is in the 1948–52 period livery of light blue as the main colour with two dark blue broad bands. 50 had been built with a Massey body and dated from September 1944, and was rebodied in November 1951 with a body formerly fitted to Dennis Lance II 120 (DDH 152), dating from 1936. Having been reseated to H30/26R when this body swap took place, 50 had a surprisingly long life and was not taken out of service until February 1963. (PM Photography)

53 (JDH 203)

Below: The Guy Arab IIs that were rebodied with pre-war Park Royal bodies and that had previously had wartime Massey bodywork could always be identified as the original Massey windscreen with its distinctively curved lower edge was salvaged and used again on the rebodied bus. 53 (JDH 203) has the 1938 body from Dennis Lance II 194 (FDH 855) and falls into the above category. It is in Bradford Place at the 38 route terminus and had only recently emerged as one of the first three buses in the fleet to wear the all-over pale blue colour scheme, and this time the three very thin bright chrome yellow livery bands clearly stand out. (R. A. Mills)

101 (JDH 256)

Above: Probably the most angular of all the products built by the coachbuilders who made wartime bus bodies were those manufactured by Massey Brothers of Pemberton. Their products were extremely variable in quality, due mainly to their stocks of wood coming from a supplier of poorly seasoned ash, which was used for the frames of their bodies. Those supplied, for instance, to London Transport were the first class of Guy Arab IIs to be taken out of service. On the other hand, many Massey-bodied vehicles, such as those operated by Ashton, Coventry and some of the Walsall examples, survived for well over eighteen years. 101 (JDH 256) lies over in Hatherton Road in the early 1950s, looking as though the 1944 livery is about to be replaced. The bus has had its wooden seats replaced by upholstered ones, but there are still only a pair of side saloon windows. This bus was rebodied in 1952 with a pre-war Park Royal body from 197 (FDH 858) and after withdrawal it was sold to Hednesford Hills Raceway, where it was used as a commentary box for the speedway events. (S. N. J. White)

105 (JDH 259)

Below: Speeding towards the town centre in about 1960 is 105 (JDH 259), a Guy Arab II which entered service in January 1945. The Corporation's new acquisitions during the Second World War were all products from Fallings Park in Wolverhampton. These were all allocated to Walsall by the Ministry of War Transport between 1942 and 1945, and the Corporation was fortunate to be able to standardise on the products of Guy Motors. 105 was bodied by Park Royal and, unlike many others in the fleet, managed to retain its original body until it was withdrawn in 1961, wearing the all-over light blue livery introduced by Mr R. Edgley Cox. It is seen beneath the wiring that took the trolleybuses to Stephenson Avenue in Stafford Street. Parked on the 'wrong' side of the road is an Austin A40, which was the 'world's first hatch-back'. Beyond it is a Hillman Husky. Following the bus is a London-registered former Post Office Morris Z-type 5 cwt van. (R. F. Mack)

36 (JDH 265)

Above: At the top of Park Street opposite the Savoy Cinema, formerly the Grand Theatre, is a steamed up 36 (JDH 265). On this rainy day the Park Royal-bodied Guy Arab II is turning into Stafford Street on its way to New Invention. The bus dated from February 1945 and survived with its wartime body intact until June 1962, and was then used as a driver training vehicle until August 1963. If the trainee could master the four-speed constant mesh gearbox, then he could drive anything. Park Street was still a town centre shopping thoroughfare, lined with largely Victorian buildings, though in later years it would be pedestrianised. (A. N. Porter)

211 (JDH 275)

Below: Originally numbered 41 (JDH 275), this was the last wartime MoWT bodied bus to be supplied to the municipality, arriving in February 1945, and originally had a Park Royal H30/26R body. Renumbered 211 it was the last of ten Guy Arab IIs to be rebodied with a new 7 foot 9 inch Willowbrook H30/26R body, which it received in January 1954. It is parked in St Paul's Street alongside the Transport offices, located at the top end of the bus station. 211 is working on the 41 service to New Invention before travelling on to Willenhall. It survived in service until July 1967. (S. N. J. White)

5

The Last of Mr Somerfield's Orders, 1948–52

The last years of Mr Somerfield's long, twenty-year tenure as General Manager were basically a continuation of his pre-war policy: build as cheaply as possible to the minimum weight, have a small engine and still maintain an intensive service both within and beyond the town. The result was that the initial post-war order for fifty buses was just a follow-on from the wartime fleet with Guy Arab IIIs with very basic Park Royal bodywork. Mr Somerfield's last new buses were twenty-five Guy Arab IIIs but with the more powerful Gardner 6LW engines and a similar number of Leyland Titan PD2/1s. They had more substantial Park Royal bodywork but, unusually, they had full fronts, which must have made maintenance more difficult.

5 (MDH 303)
Opposite above: A pair of almost new Park Royal-bodied Guy Arab IIIs with Gardner 5LW 7.0 litre engines stands at the top end of St Paul's Bus Station. 5 (MDH 303), dating from November 1948, and 110 (MDH 320), of April 1949, have worked on the 15 route to Bloxwich and the 41 to Willenhall respectively. Whereas 110 had its body extensively rebuilt in 1961, lasting until February 1967 as one of the last three of the type to remain in service, MDH 303 was the exact opposite as it was the first of these buses to be taken out of service. (A. Yates)

10 (MDH 306)
Opposite below: Waiting to load up in Bradford Place when working on the 32 route to Walstead Road is 10 (MDH 306). This Guy Arab III 5LW entered service during December 1948. The bus is in the attractive 1948 livery of all-over pale blue with two dark blue bands. The thin pillars of the Park Royal bodywork were of a style introduced in 1947 and which remained in production for about six years. 10 was renumbered 60 in December 1963 and was withdrawn in August 1966. (S. N. J. White)

28 (MDH 308)

Above: Towards the end of its long life, 28 (MDH 308) stands in Park Street alongside the side entrance of the Transport Department's offices. This Guy Arab III had entered service in December 1948 and was withdrawn exactly fifteen years later and was scrapped exactly twelve months later! It has already had its rear dome windows remounted in rubber while the waistrail around the staircase looks distinctly in need of remedial attention. The bus, painted in all-over light blue, is working on the 35 Pleck circular service. (R. H. G. Simpson)

99 (MDH 315)

Below: Wet, steamed-up and miserable – and that was only the bus crew! Walsall Corporation ran its 6 service to Sutton Coldfield, and together with West Bromwich Corporation was the only interloper into what was Midland Red territory. Until just before the Second World War double-deck operation had been forbidden in Sutton, much to the chagrin of Midland Red, which, having operated in the town since the earliest days of the company, was in dire need of extra seating capacity on its services. Walsall Corporation's first post-war order was for fifty of these MDH-registered Guy Arab III buses with Park Royal H30/26R bodies. Unlike their pre-selector gearboxed, Park Royal-bodied cousins in Wolverhampton, the Walsall vehicles had standard crash-gearboxes and the small 7.0 litre Gardner 5LW engine. 99 (MDH 315) stands outside Victoria Road Junior School in company with a Ford Anglia 100E saloon. (R. F. Mack)

100 (MDH 316)

Above: Turning right into Holyhead Road at the bottom of Lower High Street in Wednesbury is an early post-war Walsall Corporation bus. 100 (MDH 316), a Guy Arab III 5LW with a very basically trimmed Park Royal H30/26R body dating from February 1949, is working on the 37 route from Bradford Place in Walsall. On the right is the 1950s-built Lloyds Bank, which had replaced a rather stylish Victorian building, and behind it is St John's Church. On the right, outside the White Horse public house, a West Bromwich bus waits to work on the 75 service to Birmingham. (D. Wilson)

87 (MDH 318)

Below: The two-tone blue livery introduced in 1948 really enhanced the lines of the fifty Park Royal-bodied Guy Arab IIIs. 87 (MDH 318) is being used on the 23 route to Brownhills and is parked at the bottom stand in the bus station, adjacent to St Paul's Church. The bus carries a painted advertisement for the much-missed Highgate Mild Ale and it is a sad reflection that Walsall's smart bus fleet of the end of the Somerfield management era was allowed to deteriorate so badly over the last fifteen years of the municipality's independence. 87 entered service in April 1949 and remained in service until June 1965, when it was withdrawn and sold seven months later to Wombwell Diesels. (M. Rooum)

112 (MDH 321)

A large number of Walsall's 'bread and butter' services were around the many council estates that grew up in the 1930s and 1950s. At that time the policy was not for the introduction of new trolleybus services; that would come after Edgley Cox became the General Manager, who introduced the Blakenall circular route in 1955. Thus many of the outlying areas were always going to be operated by motor buses. Park Royal-bodied Guy Arab III 5LW 112 (MDH 321), dating from April 1949, works through such a housing area in Pelsall on the 12 service, which operated from Bloxwich to Walsall, via Pelsall and Rushall. (R. F. Mack)

110 (MDH 320)

Below: 110 (MDH 320) lies over at the top of St Paul's Street in about 1959. It is painted in the all-over light blue livery with the vestiges of the two chrome yellow livery lines still just visible. Park Royal-bodied Guy Arab IIIs were quite common in the West Midlands, with those owned by Wolverhampton Corporation having Gardner 6LW 8.4 litre engines and pre-selector gearboxes. The twenty owned by Midland Red had the powerful 10.35 litre six-cylinder Meadows unit whereas the Walsall ones, which had a similar-looking outline, were built to the lowest specification of all the three operators, having Gardner 5LW 7.0 litre engines and single-skinned panels. 110 was extensively rebuilt by the Corporation in 1961, which enabled it to soldier on until February 1967, but no more were rebuilt to this standard on economic grounds. (A. Yates)

109 (MDH 319)

Above: Looking much unloved towards the end of its career is 109 (MDH 319). All of these fifty Guy Arab IIIs delivered to Walsall between November 1948 and January 1950 were equipped with 7.0 litre Gardner 5LW engines, and while their H30/26R Park Royal bodies weighed only 7¾ tons, they were always underpowered, rather continuing the pre-war practice with the Dennis Lance IIs. 109 has drawn up in Bradford Place next to 221 (JDH 33), the wartime Guy Arab II cut down to a single-decker and subsequently used as a drivers' rest room and tea bar. 109 is working on the 38 route to Darlaston in early 1963, a few months before it was withdrawn. (A. D. Broughall)

244 (MDH 329)

Posed in the bright sunlight at the Park Royal coachbuilders in August 1949 prior to delivery to Walsall Corporation is 244 (MDH 329). This brand-new Guy Arab III positively gleams with its overall pale blue livery enhance by the deeper blue bands edged in black and set off with the gold, rather old-fashioned shaded fleet number. It remained in service until June 1965. (Park Royal)

248 (MDH 333)

Above: What is the collective noun for a group of buses awaiting breaking up? Perhaps a scrappage or a dumping? Whatever it might be, four Guy Arab IIIs with Park Royal H30/26R bodies have been left to their fate in scrap dealer Hoyles of Wombwell. 248 (MDH 333) had been towed to Hoyles in January 1966, having had its Gardner 5LW engine removed at Birchills Garage. The disposal of 254 (MDH 339) followed an identical path, while 4 (MDH 302), latterly numbered 54, arrived at Hoyles' yard a month later. The Walsall buses, one of which is unidentifiable, are parked with a number of former Leeds City Transport Roe-bodied AEC Regent IIIs that are awaiting a similar end. (J. Cockshott)

250 (MDH 335)

Below: On a bright sunny day at the Queen Street terminus on the 60 service, the crew of Walsall's 250 (MDH 335), a 1949 Guy Arab III 5LW with a Park Royal H30/26R body, stand in front of their charge. Despite only being about three years old, the composite bodywork around the lower saloon waistrail is beginning to show signs of unevenness. The 60 route went to Bloxwich by way of Wednesfield and New Invention. The through service was jointly operated by both Walsall and Wolverhampton Corporation and the route was divided at the Gate Inn, New Invention, with each Corporation being responsible for their section of the route on each side of the Gate. The bleak nature of the buildings reveals just how run-down this inner area of Wolverhampton was at the time. (M. Rooum)

254 (MDH 339)

Above: As the Walsall-specification bodies were lightweight to the point of being flimsy, perhaps their power-to-weight ratio was better than might have been expected. Their lifespan was variable, with the first ones being withdrawn in July 1961. Many were extensively rebuilt, as with 254 (MDH 339), seen climbing St Paul's Street when working on the 10 route to Reedswood. A white Ford Consul 204E passes the bus while travelling towards Hatherton Road. All the front dome windows have been mounted in rubber, which will stop the upper saloon from leaking but looks awful. This remedial body rebuilding allowed for 254 to stay in service in January 1966. (W. J. Haynes)

265 (MDH 350)

Below: The driver of 265 (MDH 350), parked in Bradford Place having worked on the 38 circular service, has left his cab and with his conductor has gone to the bus that served as a staff tea bar. The bus is the final one of the fifty MDH-registered Guy Arab IIIs and had entered service in January 1950. Not only was it the last of the batch to be delivered but 265 was also the last one to remain in service, not being withdrawn from PSV use until May 1967; after that it was used as a driver trainer until April 1969. (S. N. J. White)

118 (ODH 76)

Above: A further fifty buses were ordered for delivery in 1951. The body order went again to Park Royal and they were built to Mr Somerfield's specification with full-front bodies and were his swan song before his retirement. The chassis order was divided equally between twenty-five Leyland Titan PD2/1s and twenty-five Guy Arab IIIs but this time with the more powerful Gardner 6LW 8.4 litre engines. The first of the Leylands, 118 (ODH 76), stands at Platform 3 in St Paul's Bus Station in October 1952 when working on the 23 service to Brownhills via Walsall Wood. This bus was eventually withdrawn in December 1968. (D. F. Parker)

120 (ODH 78)

Below: The larger Leyland 0.600 9.8 litre engine must have been a revelation for the drivers, as for the first time in many years these buses had a surfeit of power. 120 (ODH 78) was one of the first of the Park Royal-bodied Leyland Titan PD2/1s and entered service in January 1951. This bus was transferred to West Midlands PTE on 1 October 1969 and survived for exactly two years, though it retained Walsall's livery but with fablon stickers for the legal lettering. The much rebuilt body of 120 shows distinct signs of distortion as it leaves West Bromwich Bus Station when working back to Walsall on the 14 route in 1971. (J. Carroll)

123 (ODH 81)

Above: The design of the fifty Park Royal full-front bodies had a much deeper roof line than the half-cab design of 1948 and had windows in both saloons that were more shallow. 123 (ODH 81), a Leyland Titan PD2/1, is parked at the top of St Paul's Bus Station, next to the Transport Department's bus station offices and next to the imposing sign that warns that 'BUSES ONLY ARE PERMITTED ON THIS STATION'. From the rear these fifty bodies delivered during 1951 look like fairly standard Park Royal composite construction bodies, but the nearside cab door is a suggestion of what was really different about them. (R. Marshall)

125 (ODH 83)

Below: The full-front bodies on both the Leylands and the Guys were a little anonymous with a somewhat unimaginative radiator cover embellished with five horizontal chrome slats and a strange winged device, atop which was mounted the manufacturer's badge. The full front must have been a nightmare for access to the engine for the mechanics and fitters in Birchills Garage. In May 1953, 125 (ODH 83), a Leyland Titan PD2/1, is about to work from St Paul's Bus Station to Brownhills on the 13 service. The bus is suffering from the perennial problem of a trafficator arm that has failed to return into its holder. (D. F. Parker)

131 (ODH 89)
Above: Parked in Cannock when working on the 1 route to Hednesford, while its driver talks to a possible passenger in front of the shop of Birmingham-based pork butcher Marsh & Baxter, is Guy Arab III 131 (ODH 89). One of the ways to differentiate between one of the full-front Park Royal-bodied Guy Arab IIIs and those mounted on the Leyland Titan PD2/1 was that the distance between the leading edge of the front mudguard was slightly longer on the Guys when compared to a Leyland. (D. R. Harvey Collection)

178 (ODH 97)
Below: The near side of the Park Royal full-fronted Guy Arab IIIs and the Leyland Titan PD2/1s mirrored the driver's side in that it had a sliding cab door. One would have presumed that this arrangement would be found on the contemporary trolleybus fleet but this door was mainly for the use of the garage maintenance staff. Guy Arab III 178 (ODH 97) is parked near to the exit to Birchills Garage in October 1954, while near to the garage entrance is 108 (CDH 36), a Park Royal-bodied Dennis Ace of 1935, by now being used as a ticket van. (R. F. Mack)

183 (ODH 100)

Above: Climbing up the hill in Lichfield Street with the idyllic Walsall Arboretum on the left is the heavily rebuilt Park Royal-bodied Guy Arab III 183 (ODH 100). It entered service with Walsall Corporation in February 1951 and survived into West Midlands PTE ownership to make it into its twentieth year of service. The composite-construction body was considerably modified in the mid-1960s with the fitting of rubber-mounted saloon windows. It is being employed on the 48 service to High Heath and Shelfield. 183 is being followed by 889 (889 MDH), a 30-foot-long Daimler CVG6/30 with a Metro-Cammell H41/31F forward-entrance body that had entered service in July 1961. This bus is working on the 36 service to Castlefort Estate, Walsall Wood. (R. H. G. Simpson)

217 (ODH 300)

Below: Working on the jointly operated 54 route to West Bromwich on 7 October 1965 is 217 (ODH 300), a much rebuilt Park Royal-bodied Guy Arab III. This bus had entered service in March 1951 and passed to West Midlands PTE on 1 October 1969, surviving with them until May 1971. It is turning out of New Street into High Street, West Bromwich, with the Bell & Jones chemist's and photographic shop behind 217. (A. J. Douglas)

225 (ODH 303)

Above: The one end of the long 65 bus route was in Dudley. After leaving Walsall the route, jointly operated with Midland Red, went by way of Wednesbury and Tipton to the original Dudley terminus in Tipton Road, at the junction with Birmingham Road at the bottom of Castle Hill. Here the bus was able to turn around the traffic island opposite the entrance to the Midland Red Bus Garage. Tipton Road was an important transport meeting point whose origins could be traced back to the first steam trams. As Dudley's Bus Station was not opened until 1952, a number of Midland Red and the jointly operated Birmingham-West Bromwich Corporation routes also used the Tipton Road Island as their terminus. In about 1951, the almost new Walsall Corporation 225 (ODH 303), a Guy Arab III fitted with a Gardner 6LW engine and a full-fronted, fifty-six-seater Park Royal body, is parked alongside the advertising hoardings that stood above Dudley railway station, deep in its cutting. The railway station closed on 6 July 1964 as part of Dr Beeching's cuts. (R. F. Mack)

232 (ODH 309)

Opposite below: In about 1957, before many of the old buildings in the centre of Cannock were swept away in the redevelopment that affected the town in the 1960s, are two sparkling Walsall Corporation buses. 232 (ODH 309), a 1951 Guy Arab III 6LW with a full-fronted Park Royal H30/26R body, is about to depart on the 7 service to Hednesford via Pye Green, as its driver has his finger hovering over the starter button. 232 has recently received the simplified all-blue livery, relieved with three of the thinnest chrome yellow livery bands imaginable, but it does look very smart. This bus would be withdrawn in 1967. Behind it is one of the splendid Roe-bodied Leyland Titan PD2/12s that were built in the summer of 1953. This bus is working on the 39 Cannock Circular service via Limepit Lane, which was operated jointly with Midland Red. About to overtake the two buses is a 1957 Vauxhall Victor F, a medium-sized saloon car that was the first to be built in the UK with an American-styled 'wrap-round' windscreen. They were also infamous for being readily attacked by the 'tin worm'! (R. F. Mack)

235 (ODH 807)

Above: Travelling through High Street, Chasetown, on 2 August 1954 is 235 (ODH 807). It is about to pass Chasetown's police station. Chasetown had developed in the mid-nineteenth century as a coal mining village after the first pit was sunk in 1849. As a result of the mining industry, housing for the miners began to be developed around High Street, Church Street and Queen Street. After the Second World War the Oakdene municipal estate began to be built and was still expanding by 1958, by which time Walsall Corporation was supplying most of the bus services in the Cannock area even though the last mine closed in 1959. This Leyland Titan PD2/1 had a Park Royal FH30/26R body, entering service in November 1951, and is working on the 5 service. It was a long-lived bus and was not withdrawn until May 1971, by which time it had been operating for West Midlands PTE for eighteen months. (R. Knibbs)

239 (ODH 811)

Above: On a misty morning Leyland Titan PD2/1 239 (ODH 811), which entered service in October 1951, pulls away from the two passengers it has just dropped off and continues the climb up to the traffic lights at the Shire Oak. It was here that the route crossed the A452 Chester Road. The bus is travelling towards Walsall from Lichfield and is working on the 16 service. Its Park Royal FH30/26R body is not in 'rude health' and has a considerable amount of waistrail sag. 239 would be extensively rebuilt to extend its life for another seven or so years. These powerful Leyland buses, with their 9.8 litre engines, were ideal for these long, almost inter-urban services operated by the Corporation. (R. F. Mack)

240 (ODH 812)

Below: When new ODH series buses were delivered, the main body colour was light blue, with dark blue relief in the form of two broad bands immediately above and below the lower deck windows and black lining separating the two blues, and there was an additional black band at upper deck waist level. The fleet numbers were shaded type and the fleetname was 'Walsall Corporation' in gold, with the borough crest between the two words. Leyland Titan PD2/1 240 (ODH 812) was delivered in this livery in October 1951 and was the last of the second batch of twelve with the later 8xx registration marks. It is in High Street's 'Golden Mile' in West Bromwich when working on the 214 service from Walsall via Fullbrook and Stone Cross and carries a version of the well-known early 1950s CWS and Save advertisement. (S. N. J. White)

6

1950s Single-Deckers

From 1952 nearly all the buses purchased by Walsall were 8 feet wide and those vehicles had fleet numbers in the 8xx series. However, unlike in pre-war days the use of single-deckers diminished as passenger numbers demanded larger buses. The new 1950s single-deck purchases were a mixed bag of ten underfloor-engined Leyland Royal Tiger PSU1/13s and six lightweight front-engined Bedford SBOs, which were a rarity in municipal fleets.

802 (PDH 802)
The attendance of the Walsall Corporation 1956 Morris J type van, YDH 51, operated by the transport engineers' department and the mechanic in deep discussion with the driver on the front steps of the bus suggests that all is not well with 802 (PDH 802). This was one of five Leyland Royal Tiger PSU1/13s with Leyland B44F bodies that entered service in December 1952 and was one of the first 8 foot wide buses to enter service with Walsall Corporation. The bus is in Hatherton Road and will resume its duty on the 17 route to Cannock and Cheslyn Hay. (D. R. Harvey Collection)

805 (PDH 805)

Above: Turning across St Paul's Street on its way from Hatherton Road into St Paul's Bus Station is 805 (PDH 805). Like all five of these Leyland Royal Tiger PSU1/13s with the attractive Leyland bus body characterised by its shallow roof-line, 805 passed to West Midlands PTE who quickly withdrew all of the batch and it was withdrawn in January 1972, although by that time it was reduced to a B43F layout. It is being followed by 206 (JDH 109), one of the ten Willowbrook 1953 rebodied wartime Guy Arab IIs. (D. R. Harvey Collection)

810 (PDH 810)

Above: 810 (PDH 810), new in May 1953, was a Leyland Royal Tiger PSU1/13 with a Park Royal B42F body. It has been working on the short 31 route between Bloxwich and New Invention in about 1959. These buses had the attractively designed saloon window pans, though they still had the rear centrally mounted emergency exit doors. 810 was rebuilt to DP36F with coach seats during 1961 for use as a private hire vehicle, along with 808, when the Corporation could not justify purchasing a new coach. It was subsequently repainted in a reversed livery of cream with blue lining and had its destination boxes removed. 810 passed to West Midlands PTE and remained in service until May 1973. The original order was for fifteen Leyland Tiger PS2s, but on his arrival at Walsall, Mr Edgley Cox changed the order to ten full-fronted Leyland Titan PD2/12s, to be numbered 811–820, and these five Royal Tigers. They had a fairly lightweight body construction that enabled the all-up unladen weight to be restricted to 7 tons 4 cwt. (D. R. Harvey Collection)

806 (PDH 806)

Opposite below: For many years, until the spring of 1965, Walsall Corporation could only reach as far as the notice-boards that marked the Birmingham City boundary at The Circle, Kingstanding, and no further! This was when their buses were working on the 50 or 58 services from Bloxwich or Aldridge. Walsall Corporation's 806 (PDH 806) waits in Kingstanding Road, just outside the operational area of Birmingham Corporation. 806 is working on the 50 route, which will take it back to Bloxwich by way of Aldridge and Pelsall. The single-decker is a Leyland Royal Tiger PSU1/13 and had a Park Royal B42F body. It had entered service in May 1953 and was converted to OMO in December 1961. (D. Williams)

294 (XDH 294)

Above: An unusual purchase in January 1956 was of five Bedford SBOs with 7 ft 6 in. wide Willowbrook B39F bodies. The buses had prominent front destination boxes and although they only had a life of barely eleven years, they led fairly quiet lives on the more rural routes in the Bloxwich area and were used on routes with low bridges. 294 (XDH 294) is standing in St Paul's Bus Station when about to work on the 55 route to Aldridge by way of Rushall. (A. D. Broughall)

298 (XDH 298)

Below: 298 (XDH 298), a Bedford SBO with a Perkins R6 6.354 litre Diesel engine that had a reputation for being somewhat unreliable, stands in Birchills Garage yard. The Willowbrook B39F body was supplied to the Corporation at a time when the Loughborough-based coachbuilder was the favoured body provider. These buses had an attractively low window line in front of the front axle, which would have aided the driver when loading up passengers. After withdrawal in December 1967, 298 became yet another mobile canteen (oh, how the crews must have enjoyed their mugs of tea!) and was eventually withdrawn by WMPTE in June 1973. (D. R. Harvey Collection)

7

Mid-1950s Double-Deckers

This was the age of Ronald Edgley Cox, which could only be described as idiosyncratic. Throughout the 1950s his motor bus purchases, with the exception of the batches of Roe-bodied Leyland Titan PD2/12s of 1953 and the fifteen Daimler CVG6s with Willowbrook bodies of 1956, were usually one-off prototypes characterised by lightweight bodies and, where possible, small capacity engines. In some respects this had always been the policy of Walsall's management ever since the later 1920s, but the new incumbent took it to a new level. A very simplified all-over light blue livery with the thinnest of chrome yellow bands was introduced. Meanwhile, during the 1950s, as well as a solitary experimental Sunbeam S7A six-wheel trolleybus, a total of twenty-two Willowbrook-bodied Sunbeam F4A trolleybuses were purchased for the new Blakenhall service opened for 1955 and the Beechdale route in 1956. These were the first PSVs built to this length in the United Kingdom and paved the way for 30-foot, two-axle, double-decker motorbuses to be operated – a type that, needless to report, Walsall enthusiastically bought.

811 (RDH 501)
There cannot be too many buses that can claim to be the products of three different coachbuilders but 811–813 could! Leyland Titan PD2/12s 811–3 were lengthened to 28 ft 11 in., with a slightly increased rear overhang, and the original Park Royal metal-framed Roe bodywork was converted by Willowbrook to forward entrance, becoming FH39/32F. The first of these conversions to be completed was 811 (RDH 501), in August 1959. Freshly back from its rebuilding, 811 is in St Paul's Bus Station when working on the 34 route to Rushall and Westgate. (A. D. Broughall)

812 (RDH 502)

Above: Parked in Birchills Garage yard, the nearside of 812 (RDH 502) shows how an extra half bay was inserted by Willowbrook into the bodywork of the existing structure, behind the repositioned forward entrance in the lower saloon and in front of the front upper saloon bay. The result was quite neat, but with the new windows mounted in rubber and not, as with the rest of the bus, in proper window pans, it did have an Eccles Caravan look about the conversion! This Leyland Titan PD2/12 had entered service in July 1953, was converted to forward entrance in January 1960 by Willowbrook and was withdrawn by WMPTE in June 1971. (D. R. Harvey Collection)

816 (RDH 506)

Below: Parked in a very wet Queen Street in Wolverhampton's town centre in April 1959 is 816 (RDH 506), one of the Roe-bodied FH30/23RD Leyland Titan PD2/12s of July 1953. This was one of the buses that retained its original length although it was re-seated to FH30/26RD. The somewhat hangdog frontal appearance is not helped by horizontal chrome bars over the radiator cowling, which does look marginally better than the frontal appearance of the fifty ODH-registered double-deckers but makes them look vaguely like a Foden. (D. F. Parker)

817 (RDH 507)

Above: 811–20 were Leyland Titan PD2/12s built to the then maximum dimensions of 27 feet long and 8 feet wide. They had special provision for extra luggage accommodation, thus having the low capacity of only twenty-three seats in the lower saloon. They also had a forced air system as well as the normal sliding ventilators. They were also the first double-deck vehicles to appear in the new Walsall livery of light blue with chrome yellow lining. They were to have been built with Park Royal bodies but the body order was subcontracted to Roe. The only other vaguely similar Leyland PD2/12s with a full front and a Roe/Park Royal body were the double-deck coaches supplied to East Yorkshire Road Car. 817 is parked in front of the main office building of Charles Roe prior to delivery in June 1953, hence the elaborate flag to celebrate the Coronation of HRH Queen Elizabeth II. (Roe)

818 (RDH 508)

Below: 818 (RDH 508) is leaving St Paul's Bus Station on the 56 route to Aldridge. This Leyland Titan PD2/12 had not been lengthened but was one of three of the class to have the seating capacity increased by three in the lower saloon to FH33/26R by the removal of luggage racks. As with many classes of bus that various operators modified, this unrebuilt bus benefitted from retaining its original form and became one of the last three to remain in service, having been transferred to West Midland PTE. It was in full WMPTE livery of Oxford blue and cream and was finally withdrawn in June 1973. (A. J. Douglas)

826 (WDH 901)

Above: Such were the numbers of buses that used St Paul's Bus Station that other nearby lay-over sites were required. One such site was Hatherton Road, to the right of the parked buses, and also at St Paul's Close, where there was a small patch of vacant land parallel to St Paul's Street on the extreme left. 826 and 827 (WDH 901–2), the first two of the low-highbridge Willowbrook-bodied Daimler CVG6s, were delivered in March 1956, and unusually for their time, were equipped with platform doors. The inset upper saloon front windows on these bodies were a feature that supplied fresh air through ventilators in the front dome. Both buses passed to West Midlands PTE, with 826 being withdrawn in October 1972 while 827 became a driver trainer for nine months after it was withdrawn as a PSV in July 1974. (Photobus)

833 (WDH 908)

Below: Just pulling away from the bus shelter in Cannock Bus Station on 15 May 1969 is 833 (WDH 908). This was one of the 826–840 batch of Daimler CVG6s delivered between March and May 1956 and again showed the General Manager's willingness to adopt new ideas. The buses were built to the same specification as the well-known Daimler demonstrator, SDU 711. These buses all had Twiflex couplings that enabled the usual fluid flywheel to be replaced with a conventional friction clutch while retaining an automatic gear selection. Daimler's intention was to try to woo orders from operators who were wedded to synchromesh gearboxes and rarely ordered Daimlers. It was hardly a success and the Walsall order represented the largest batch ever to be built. (A. J. Douglas)

834 (WDH 909)

Above: Passing beneath the old Stone Cross Bridge that carries the Tame Valley Canal aqueduct at The Navigation Inn, in Navigation Lane, is Daimler CVG6 834 (WDH 909). Their Willowbrook H37/29R bodies were built to a 'low-highbridge' height of 14 feet and were suitable to clear low bridges such as this one. This was achieved by building the body directly on to the chassis frame with outrigger supports and not using the usual body underframing; the lower body height is indicated by the way the top of the driver's cab door intrudes into the panels between the decks. (D. Wilson)

837 (WDH 912)

Below: When 'fresh out of the box', 837 (WDH 912) is parked at the terminus of the jointly operated 14 route in Lower Queen Street, opposite the front of the King's Cinema in West Bromwich. This terminus for the jointly operated 14 and 54 routes by Walsall and West Bromwich Corporations had only been in use since 20 September 1954. 837 is loading up prior to departing for Walsall in April 1956. A brand new 837, a Daimler CVG6 with a Willowbrook H37/29RD body, entered service in April 1956. These buses could be identified as being low-height by their lower saloon waistrails being lower than the normal depth windscreen. The four bay construction Willowbrook bodies were built on the chassis outriggers, resulting in the bodies being lower height but with a standard upper saloon layout. These buses originally had Twiflex centrifugal clutches and were nicknamed 'jumping jacks' due to their bouncy suspension and lively handling. (D. Williams)

840 (WDH 915)

Approaching St Paul's Bus Station from Hatherton Road is 840 (WDH 915), the last of the fifteen Willowbrook H37/29R-bodied Daimler CVG6s. Well loaded with passengers, the bus heels over on its springs as it turns right into St Paul's Street. Their suspension was – to say the least – lively, as suggested by the angle of the bodywork, and they were given the nickname 'jumping jacks' as conductors found it difficult to stand on the rear platform or to take the fares from seated passengers. It is working on the 1 route from Hednesford, Cannock and Bloxwich into Walsall. Behind the large Austin A70 Herford Countryman coming out of St Paul's Street is the small bus parking lot for buses awaiting a loading spot in the bus station. (L. Mason)

Demonstrators, 'One-Offs' and Lightweights

Demonstrators came and went with amazing rapidity, with many being exhibited at that year's Commercial Motor Show at Earl's Court. With this added publicity for the Corporation the policy remained that there was always the view of finding something lighter. A number were eventually purchased by the Corporation after a successful trial, though rarely did any orders accrue from the demonstration.

NTF 9
NTF 9 was the only Leyland Titan PD2/15 to be built. It was a 27-foot-long and 8-foot-wide chassis but was fitted with an experimental epicyclic gearbox. It also had one of the later Leyland bodies with rounded window pans and had a standard H30/26R seating layout. It was demonstrated periodically between November 1955 and about February 1957. NTF 9 is parked in Green Lane alongside the 1936-built Art Deco-styled ABC Cinema as The Savoy. The cinema is showing *The Man in the Road*, which was released in the spring of 1956. It was a British Cold War spy thriller film starring Derek Farr, Ella Raines, Donald Wolfit and Cyril Cusack about a brilliant scientist suffering from amnesia who is hunted by Communist agents in search of a secret formula. The bus is about to depart for Hednesford. (D. R. Harvey Collection)

PHP 220

Above: PHP 220 was originally built as the fourth prototype CL experimental lightweight chassis in 1952. It was subsequently bodied by Northern Counties with a H33/28R body and was first registered for use as a demonstrator in 1954. By the time it went on loan to Walsall Corporation for just one month from November to December 1955, although it still retained some lightweight features, it was redesignated as a CVG6. It was sold to Burwell & District in March 1956 and is parked in Cambridge Bus Station in about 1960. (D. R. Harvey Collection)

400 (TDH 99)

Below: The bodywork on 400 (TDH 99) was built as a 7 ft 6 in. wide Northern Counties to virtually the same design as that on PHP 220, although the seating capacity was slightly reduced to H32/28R. It entered service in June 1954 and was a Daimler CVG5, being the first bus built to Mr Edgley Cox's new policy to introduce into the fleet small-engined, lightweight-bodied vehicles and was probably the best looking of all the Daimlers bought at this time. 400 (TDH 99) turns out of the bottom end of St Paul's Bus Station when working on the 16 route to Lichfield via Walsall Wood. (D. R. Harvey)

400 (TDH 99)

Above: Travelling past Walsall Arboretum in Lichfield Street, 400 (TDH 99), the Northern Counties-bodied Daimler CVG5, travels into Walsall to terminate in St Paul's Bus Station when it was about seven years old. The bus became 400L when taken over by WMPTE in October 1969, and although it was never repainted into their Oxford blue and cream livery, it stayed in service until September 1971. (R. Hannay)

401 (YDH 401)

Below: Metal Sections supplied a lot of double-deck body frames during the mid-1950s to numerous municipal operators, including Belfast and Merthyr Tydfil. These were completed by local coachbuilders who certainly made the buses look more attractive than the one completed by Walsall Corporation in November 1956 on Daimler CVG5 401 (YDH 401). The internal finish was extremely spartan and the external detail design work left a lot to be desired, with rubber gasket mounted windows and the angled front windows with concealed ventilation slats below the dome. It is parked alongside the Dennis Ace tea bar in Bradford Place having worked on the 38 route from Darlaston. (D. R. Harvey Collection)

401 (YDH 401)

Above: In the early 1960s one of Walsall Corporation's more eccentric vehicles, 401 (YDH 401), built to the lightweight specifications of Mr Edgley Cox, stands at the bus shelters in Lower High Street, Wednesbury, with New Street disappearing down the hill towards Potters Lane and the former GWR railway station. 401 is a Daimler CVG5 fitted with a five-cylinder 7.0 litre Gardner 5LW engine rather than the more usual post-war standard Gardner 6LW unit. The gaunt-looking body was built at Birchills Garage using metal section frames manufactured in Oldbury. This lightweight bus entered service in November 1956 and lasted into West Midlands PTE days. (D. R. Harvey Collection)

821 (TDH 673)

Below: 821 (TDH 673) had been designated as a Daimler CLG5 as it had some lightweight chassis springing, but after only two completed vehicles, REH 500 for PMT and LOG 302 for Birmingham City Transport, the model was quietly dropped and so 821 acquired a CVG5 chassis plate. The bus had a very similar Northern Counties body to that fitted to 400 (TDH 99), although the seating capacity was increased to H37/28R. It is parked in Birchills Garage yard when about ten years old. (D. R. Harvey Collection)

821 (TDH 673)

Above: Pretending to be a trolleybus, 821 (TDH 673) works on the 30 route to Bloxwich. It is pulling out of St Paul's Bus Station as it travels out of the town centre to Townend. Behind and alongside it are a couple of the 1956-built Willowbrook-bodied Sunbeam F4A trolleybuses, standing at the shelters in the bus station. It was exhibited at the October 1954 Commercial Motor Show at Earl's Court before entering service immediately afterwards. 821 was taken over by WMPTE and was withdrawn in June 1973. (J. Cockshott)

822 (TDH 769)

Below: Parked in Carl Street alongside Birchills Garage is AEC Regent V MD2RA 822 (TDH 769). This was the second MD3RV chassis to be built and had an AV470 7.6 litre AEC engine. When new it was demonstrated at the 1954 Commercial Motor Show at Earl's Court before arriving in Walsall in October 1954. Despite being a one-off in the Walsall fleet it managed nearly seventeen years in service. Dumped alongside it at the end of the terrace of 1920s municipal hoses is the long withdrawn Dennis E 55 (DH 5505), whose chassis dated from 1926 and which had received a new W. D. Smith B32R body and was used as a towing vehicle until as late as October 1963. (L. Mason)

822 (TDH 769)

Above: 822 (TDH 769) was an AEC Regent V MD2RA. This was a lightweight version of the Regent V and had a Monocontrol fluid flywheel epicyclic gearbox and air brakes, which fitted in well with the Walsall trials to produce as light a bus as would be possible. The bus had a new style of concealed radiator with a grill similar to a 1954 Rover 60. 822 had a Park Royal sixty-one-seat body that weighed only 6½ tons. The body design, particularly at the rear end, had a certain similarity to the London Transport RTs. The bus is loading up with passengers in Green Lane alongside the 1936-built ABC Cinema, which is showing the 1958 film *The Brothers Karamazov*. This drama was based on Dostoevsky's homonymous novel about the proud Karamazov family in the Russia of the 1870s and starred Yul Brynner, Maria Schell and Claire Bloom. (Travel Lens)

823 (TDH 770)

Below: Parked outside the Earl's Court exhibition centre is Leyland Titan PD2/20, which was a model with vacuum brakes and a synchromesh gearbox. Its window posters advertise that the Metro-Cammell Orion Mark IV body had patented metal construction bodywork. In its exhibition condition at the 1954 Commercial Motor Show, the body appeared to be of a fairly robust lightweight design, but within months of entering service it required a lot of remedial strengthening work to prevent the structure from flexing. (D. R. Harvey Collection)

823 (TDH 770)

Above: Working along West Bromwich High Street on the way out of town on the 14 service back to Walsall by way of Stone Cross during 1955 is the nearly new double-decker 823 (TDH 770). This was a Leyland Titan PD2/20 with a very lightweight Metro-Cammell H32/28R body that had entered service in October 1954 after having been an exhibit at the 1954 Commercial Motor Show. Behind the bus is pre-war West Bromwich Corporation 97 (AEA 27), a Daimler COG5 with a Metro-Cammell H30/26R body that was one of the new bus fleet that replaced the Birmingham City Transport trams on the Dudley and Wednesbury routes in April 1939. 97 was withdrawn in December 1956 while 823 lasted until June 1973 and was the only one of the three 1954 Commercial Motor Show buses bought by Walsall to be repainted in the new WMPTE livery. (D. Williams)

800 (STF 90)

Below: Having been given the temporary number 800 in the Walsall Corporation fleet, STF 90, the Leyland Lowloader LTN with a Saunders-Roe FH37/24R body, stands at the Stone Cross Public House during 1956. It is working on the 14 service, which took the direct route between Walsall and West Bromwich, crossing the Tame Valley and reaching the Broadway in Walsall at the Fullbrook Public House. Behind 800 is an unidentified pre-war West Bromwich Corporation Daimler COG6 double-decker, which is turning from Walsall Road into Hall Green Road. This strange trolleybus-like experimental Lowloader was the first ever attempt to produce a rear-engined double-decker. Although it had an open rear platform, the Leyland O.350 engine was mounted transversely across the very rear of the bus and the engine compartment's ventilation slats are visible behind the staircase. The bus was demonstrated by Leyland Motors to Walsall for over a year, with the Corporation being a willing participant in the operation of this test bed. The Stone Cross pub dates from the 1920s, and stands at the junction of Hall Green Road and Walsall Road. The whole area was built up in the 1920s and 1930s with mainly semi-detached housing. (D. Williams)

824 (YDH 224)

Above: 824 (YDH 224) was the third Daimler CVG6/30 to be built, and other than its Willowbrook-bodied twin, the demonstrator VKV 99, it was the only one to have a Birmingham-styled 'New Look' concealed radiator cowl. The chassis had the longer 18 ft 6 in. wheelbase version of the standard post-war double-decker and was designed to take advantage of the change in UK legislation allowing for the first time 30-foot-long double-deckers to operate on two axles. It was equipped with a Gardner 6LW 8.4 litre engine and a Wilson pre-selector gearbox coupled to a Daimler fluid flywheel. 824 is in Green Lane during September 1963 when working on the 1 route from Hednesford, Cannock and Bloxwich into Walsall, where its seventy-three-seat capacity was very useful for this busy long distance service. (D. F. Parker)

824 (YDH 224)

Below: Willowbrook-bodied Daimler CVG6/30 was exhibited at the 1956 Commercial Motor Show and entered service with Walsall in February 1957. Its body was very similar in general design to the 1956 batch of 27-foot-long Daimler CVG6s and to the twenty-two 30-foot-long Sunbeam F4A trolleybuses delivered between 1954 and 1956. 824 was transferred to West Midlands PTE on 1 October 1969 as 824L and was withdrawn in June 1973. It is parked in the bus lay-over carriageway in St Paul's Street in West Midlands ownership in about September 1970. (Travel Lens)

825 (YDH 225)

Above: One of the stars of the 1956 Commercial Motor Show was the Crossley-bodied Crossley Bridgemaster MB3RA, 825 (YDH 225), which was exhibited on the Crossley stand. This 30-foot-long, 7 ton 11 cwt bus was only 13 ft 5 in. tall but was underpowered, being equipped with the small AEC AV470 7.58 litre engine and a four-speed synchromesh gearbox. Proudly wearing its Crossley Coptic Cross badge on the radiator, 825 is parked at the Transport Office end of St Paul's Bus Station when still quite new, having worked into Walsall on the 5 route from Hednesford by way of Chasetown. (R. Marshall)

825 (YDH 225)

Below: In the mid-1950s Walsall Corporation seemed to attract oddments and one-offs like bees to a honey-pot. Their General Manager, Mr Edgley Cox, had a liking for the unusual, unique and eye-catching. Between 1954 and 1958, no fewer than six of Walsall's new buses appeared at the Earl's Court Commercial Motor Show, including the first of the five Crossley-bodied Crossley Bridgemaster MB3RAs. Despite the initial enthusiasm for rear entrance, front-engined 30-foot-long buses as fulfilled by 824 (the Daimler CVG6/30) and 825, the Crossley remained Walsall's only Bridgemaster. Still sporting Crossley's Coptic Cross badge on the top of the front grill, 825 (YDH 225) is parked over the pits in Birchills Garage, a place it frequented all too often! (L. Mason)

841 (841 FDH)

Above: The only rear-engined Leyland Atlantean PDR1/1 to be purchased was 841 (841 FDH). This was perhaps a surprise, bearing in mind Mr Edgley Cox's penchant for the unusual. The first production Atlanteans had only entered service in December 1959 and this bus was delivered to Walsall in September 1959. It had Weymann L40/34F bodywork which, because of the straight back axle, had a raised rear seating the section in order to retain the necessary legal height in the lower saloon. These early low-height Weymann bodies could always be identified by low-height lower saloon windows. The raised rows of seats are just visible as the almost new 841 waits to leave the Ogley Hay terminus on the 23 route. (D. R. Harvey Collection)

841 (841 FDH)

Below: The rear-engined Leyland Atlantean PDR1/1 was a very mechanically advanced bus with such complexities as an electrically operated pneumocyclic gearbox, a centrifugal clutch and a transversely mounted Leyland 9.8 litre o.600 engine. 841 (841 FDH) passed to West Midlands PTE in October 1969 and was converted to OMO in October 1972. It remained in service until February 1977. It is parked in St Paul's Street, near to the bus station, and is wearing the Oxford blue and cream livery of the PTE. (D. R. Harvey)

9

Second-Hand Purchases

In 1959 there were two notable separate second-hand purchases: two lowbridge Leyland Titan PD1As for a service that had previously been operated by single-deckers, and five cheaply purchased former London Transport Leyland RTLs, four of which were just over five years old, were acquired. Mr Edgley Cox's past experience at St Helens included the only purchases outside London for two groups of virtually standard AEC Regent III 0961RT types, so the acquisition of these five similarly bodied RTLs was a distinct link with his past. Mr Cox had offered to purchase a batch of LTE six-wheel QI trolleybuses about this time, but the five RTLs were as close as he could get to buying former London Transport buses.

198 (EED 9)
Standing in Church Street, Cannock, on 15 August 1959 is 198 (EED 9), just two months after it was acquired. With its freshly painted light blue livery, the bus is alongside the churchyard of the twelfth-century St Luke's Parish Church, enlarged in the fourteenth century with the addition of nave arcades and the tower. 198, a Leyland Titan PD1A, was originally owned by Warrington Corporation, and was new in October 1947. It was acquired in June 1959 and was withdrawn in March 1963. (A. J. Douglas)

199 (EED 10)

Above: Having just passed the Town Hall in Lichfield Street is Leyland Titan PD1A 199 (EED 10), which is working on the service to Aldridge not long after being purchased. It had been built in 1947 and was purchased, along with EED 9, in 1959 from Warrington Corporation, where it had been numbered 101. The two buses had lowbridge fifty-three-seater Air Dispatch bodies on East Lancs frames and were purchased for the routes where there was insufficient clearance beneath bridges. Parked on the left, in front of offices occupying some formerly quite grand early Victorian houses, is a Morris Oxford and a Standard 10, both of which are only three or four years old. (L. Mason)

202 (NXP 956)

Below: Mr R. Edgley Cox had previously been the General Manager of St Helen's Corporation, and was responsible for the purchase of the only AEC Regent III RT types built with standard London Transport Park Royal-style bodies outside the capital. Fifteen were built in May to June 1950 and another twenty-five were delivered in 1952. It therefore came as no real surprise that in 1958, when the first of the LTE RTL class of Leyland Titan 7RTs were withdrawn, he managed to purchase five of these fairly new but redundant buses. The bargain was that other than the first one, 201, which dated from 1950, the other four were only five years old. 202 (NXP 956), formerly RTL 1470, stands alongside the Transport Department's offices in St Paul's Street soon after entering service in September 1959. It has been freshly repainted in the all-over light blue livery and still retains the LT-style rear wheel discs and destination box layout. (D. R. Harvey Collection)

204 (OLD 601)

Above: 204 (OLD 601), formerly RTL 1492 in the London Transport fleet and new in April 1954, was a bargain when purchased when only five years old. It is pulling away from the shelters in St Paul's Street and is about to cross the road and go onto the parking lot opposite the distant bus station. The bus has been working on the long 17 route from Cheslyn Hay. By now the destination box layout had been modified with the route number and destination rubber mounted aperture being in use. This bus eventually passed to West Midlands PTE and was withdrawn in September 1971 without ever receiving the PTE blue and cream livery. (D. R. Harvey Collection)

205 (OLD 603)

Below: 201–205 were basically Leyland-engined versions of the Park Royal-bodied RTs that Edgley Cox had purchased new when he had been the GM at St Helens. A passenger talks to the conductor of a rather battered looking 205 (OLD 603), whose driver is about to pull away from the shelters in Cannock Bus Station as he starts the last section of the route from Cannock Bus Station to Cheslyn Hay in about 1965. This bus was withdrawn in February 1968. (R. F. Mack)

10

The 1960s Forward Entrance Fleet

At the very end of the decade, Dennis Brothers were approached by Mr Cox to build a forward-entrance Loline low-height bus which pre-dated the Bristol Lodekka equivalent from which the Loline had been derived. A trial bus was built and a further fifteen of this Mark II model were bought; then, yet again, the purchasing policy was altered and 30-foot-long forward-entrance Daimler CVG6/30s and AEC Regent Vs briefly held sway in 1961.

800 (600 DDH)
800 (600 DDH) was the first Dennis Loline II YF1 to be built. This was a modified Loline I but with a chassis, albeit still a development of the Bristol Lodekka, designed to accept forward-entrance bodywork. This development had been suggested by Mr Edgley Cox. Fitted with a Willowbrook H41/29F body, it was exhibited at the 1958 Commercial Motor Show. It entered service with Walsall Corporation in January 1959, but was then borrowed by Dennis Brothers to act as a demonstrator to Edinburgh for about a month from 8 April 1959. It is being used on the Edinburgh Corporation 19 Circle service in St Andrew Square, one of the city's many early nineteenth-century lined squares. (A. S. Bronn)

SWS 261

Above: 261 (SWS 261), a Leyland Titan PD3/3 with an Alexander H41/31F body, was on loan for about one month from Edinburgh Corporation Transport, arriving in Walsall on 8 April 1959. Retaining its Edinburgh fleet number, 261, it was demonstrated to Walsall in exchange for Dennis Loline 800 (800 DDH). It is just leaving St Paul's Bus Station when working on the 5 route to Hednesford, just north-east of Cannock, on one of Walsall's longest routes. (R. H. G. Simpson)

843 (243 HDH)

Below: The Dennis Loline II YF2 was based on the Bristol Lodekka but the Loline Mark II, built to Walsall's specification, predated the forward-entrance FLF model by a few months. The nearside of the chassis of the original Loline was reworked to provide a single-step entrance with a gently ramped lower saloon floor. Parked at the top end of St Paul's Bus Station is 843 (243 HDH). It is parked with its front sliding door left open, which reveals the single-step entrance but not the awkward position of the gearbox casing, which slightly obstructed the access to the front staircase. The Willowbrook body on this had a useful seating capacity for seventy-four passengers. (R. Marshall)

845 (245 HDH)

Above: Travelling towards Townend Bank on the 7 route to Hednesford is 845 (245 HDH). The bus is in the ownership of WMPTE but is still in the Corporation's former all-over light blue livery with fablon legal lettering stickers. Withdrawals began in May 1970 and concluded in December 1974 with 845. The first four of these Willowbrook-bodied buses all survived into 1974, having been given a major overhaul at Birchills Garage before the decision was made that it would be uneconomic to pursue the idea with the rest of the batch. (D. R. Harvey Collection)

846 (246 HDH)

Below: Parked next to the 1950s public toilets in Park Road, Bloxwich, and in front of the Bull's Head Public House is Dennis Loline II YF2 846 (246 HDH). Powered by an 8.4 litre Gardner 6LW engine through a constant mesh gearbox, the low-height Willowbrook H44/30F body accentuates the length of the bus, as does the 18 ft 6 in. wheelbase. The bus is lying over when working on the Bloxwich–New Invention–Willenhall service. On resuming its duty, 846 will move off and cross the High Street, Bloxwich, and travel along Wolverhampton before reaching Sneyd Lane and travelling to New Invention. (T. W. W. Knowles)

848 (248 HDH)
Above: Despite their difficult driving characteristics, which included a very awkward five-speed constant mesh gearbox and oddly angled steering column, the Dennis Loline IIs remained in service after the West Midlands PTE took over. They were painted in the blue and cream livery of the PTE. 848 (248 HDH) is parked in Birchills Garage, along with 846, 842, 844, 847 and the prototype 800 and the one off Leyland Titan PD2/20 lightweight 823 (TDH 770). All the Mark II Lolines passed to West Midlands PTE, which in view of their 'stick' change gearbox was perhaps surprising. (J. Haddock)

878 (878 HDH)
Below: Loaded up to nearly its complete capacity of passengers in St Paul's Bus Station is Dennis Loline II YF2 878 (878 HDH). This bus, with its Willowbrook H44/30F body, is about to leave for Hednesford on the 23 route. The distant trolleybuses are standing in St Paul's Street, from where all the trolleybus routes, numbered 30/15, 31, 32 and 33 going to Bloxwich, Lower Farm and the Beechdale Estate, departed. The original trolleybus route to Wolverhampton started from Townend Street and coincidentally, like its Oporto counterpart in Portugal, which also had the route number 29, was totally isolated from the town's major trolleybus departure point. 878 entered service in March 1960 with a slightly different registration number sequence to those in the first seven and was withdrawn by West Midlands PTE in May 1972. (D. Williams)

881 (881 HDH)

Above: Climbing Lichfield Street from the junction with Littleton Street, when working on the 23 service to Brownhills, is one of Walsall Corporation's forward-entrance, Willowbrook-bodied Dennis Loline II YF2s, 881 (HDH 881), fitted with a Gardner 8.4 litre engine. To the left is Walsall Arboretum, first opened on 2 May 1874 on a ninety-nine-year lease from Lord Hatherton on land that had been a flooded limestone working. After years of losing money, the Arboretum was bought by the Corporation for £4,600 and was finally opened as a free public park on 21 July 1884. Today it is one of Walsall's treasures, with a large variety of species of trees in mature groves and stands. (D. Williams)

883 (883 HDH)

Below: The brand-new Dennis Loline II YF2 had a Gardner 6LW 8.4 litre engine and a Willowbrook H44/30F body and this one is parked in St Paul's Street, facing Townend. 883 (883 HDH) had entered service in March 1960. In view of Mr Edgley Cox's repeated requests to Dennis to develop a Loline forward-entrance chassis, which they did in six weeks, it must have been disappointing for the Guildford-based company that Walsall only ordered a total of just seventeen of the Mark II model. A 1957 Ford Popular pulls out to overtake 883, with a line-up of parked buses behind the car including 841, the solitary Leyland Atlantean. 883 would be the last Dennis Loline II to remain in service and was not withdrawn until October 1972. (R. Hannay)

885 (885 HDH)

Above: Walsall Corporation ran a large number of colliery services in the Cannock Chase and Great Wyrley areas, and although never very remunerative, they at least provided a regular income for the Corporation as its bread and butter work. The 115 service was one of these, running from Walsall to Bloxwich in normal service, but then going on to the Wyrley No. 3 Colliery. Standing among the colliery buildings in a black, wet landscape is the solitary Dennis Loline Mk II, YF10 885 (885 LDH), delivered new to Walsall. This forward-entrance Willowbrook-bodied bus had been an exhibit at the 1960 Commercial Motor Show and differed from the rest of Walsall's Lolines by having rear-axle air suspension. It is being employed on an enthusiasts' tour of the routes around Cannock. (L. Mason)

886 (MDH 886)

Below: Travelling along Coalpool Lane in July 1963, 886 (MDH 886) is working on the 49 route to Bloxwich from Walsall by way of Blakenhall and Goscote. It is following the trolleybus wires used by the 15 and 30 routes. 886 was a Daimler CVG6/30 fitted with a forward-entrance MCCW seventy-two-seater body. The chassis of 886 was built to CSD6/30 specification with a four-speed synchromesh gearbox and was exhibited at the Commercial Motor Show and the 1959 Scottish Motor Show; it was re-engined with a Gardner 6LW engine and a Wilson pre-selector gearbox before it was sent to Metro-Cammell for bodying and subsequently was sold to Walsall Corporation Transport, who registered the bus in August 1961. (D. F. Parker)

887 (MDH 887)

Above: By now renumbered 887L, 887 MDH travels into Walsall on the 302 route. Delivered to Walsall in August 1961, this Metro-Cammell H41/31F-bodied Daimler CVG6/30 lasted until January 1977 with WMPTE. It has received the standard WMPTE Oxford blue and cream livery with the added luxury of being repainted at Walsall Works and therefore having the addition of the mid-deck thin blue line. It was perhaps surprising that Walsall did not order any more than this batch of five, especially as the neighbouring municipality of West Bromwich took thirty-five examples of the Daimler CVG6/30. (D. R. Harvey Collection)

888 (888 MDH)

Below: Still wearing its full Walsall livery although the Walsall crests have been covered by the WM WEST MIDLANDS fablon stickers, the bus surprisingly still retains its Walsall fleet number. 888 (888 MDH) is parked in St Paul's Bus Station when working on the 6 route to Aldridge and Sutton Coldfield a short time after the PTE took over the operations of Walsall Corporation. These buses only had the Garner 6 LW 8.4 litre engine and must have been at their limit of performance, especially on demanding services such as this one. (D. R. Harvey Collection)

891 (891 MDH)

Above: Birmingham's subterranean Bull Ring Centre Bus Station had opened on 3 November 1963 and was used extensively by Midland Red for all their Stage Carriage Services. It was, however, not a passenger-friendly place! Walsall Corporation began using the facility after they became joint operators of the 118 route with Midland Red. Metro-Cammell-bodied AEC Regent V 891 (891 MDH) lies over after arriving in Birmingham on the 118 service. On the day when the Walsall bus was parked in the bus station it looked well-lit with extensive fluorescent lighting and ample room. In reality it was an exhaust-filled, claustrophobic location with poor passenger facilities and was difficult to reach, being just on the fringe of the city centre. At weekends it was a nightmare for drivers to get their buses in, load and depart without meeting congestion from other vehicles. (D. R. Harvey Collection)

892 (892 MDH)

Below: Unlike the Dennis Loline IIs, the AEC Regent chassis shows its deficiency in the low-height stakes. Parked in St Paul's Bus Station after working on the 4 service from Heath Hayes and Brownhills, with the sliding doors of its Metro-Cammell body open the two-step entrance into the lower saloon is revealed. 892 (892 MDH) had the same body configuration as the previous batch of five Daimler CVG6/30s, which had also entered service in August 1961. They had marginally shorter operational lives than the Daimlers, with 892 being withdrawn in July 1975. (R. H. G. Simpson)

893 (893 MDH)

Above: Working on the 47 service between Walsall, Lichfield and Cannock in 1961 is an almost new, advert-free AEC Regent V 2D2RA, with a Metro-Cammell H41/31F body. These semi-automatic Mono-Control buses had the AV590 9.6 litre engine and thus had a pleasantly sophisticated chassis. It was a shame that they were ordered with the lowest specification MCCW Orion body. They were the last 30-foot-long, half-cab, front-engined double-decker buses bought by the Corporation earlier in the same summer. Standing in The Friary, Lichfield, is 893 (893 MDH). (R. F. Mack)

896 (896 MDH)

Below: Standing in the centre of Cannock, beneath the trees alongside the large fourteenth-century Parish Church of St Luke, is brand-new 896 (896 MDH), the first of the five Willowbrook seventy-two-seater AEC Regent V 2D2RAs that entered service in August 1961. They were numerically the last 30-foot-long half-cabs to enter service with Walsall Corporation and 896 is working on the Cannock and Limepit Lane circular service. About to overtake the bus is a Commer Superpoise Super Capacity van, which was more usually known simply as the 30 cwt, being used by Taylor's, a local bakery, as a delivery van. (R. F. Mack)

899 (899 MDH)

Above: Well over half the services operated by Walsall Corporation were outside the town's boundaries. This vast operating area extended not only into the Black Country but also into the area to the north and east of the town, reaching outposts such as Lichfield, Rugeley, Stafford and Cannock. About to leave the bleak concrete bus shelters that were on Cannock Bus Station is Willowbrook-bodied AEC Regent V 2D2RA 899 (899 MDH). The bus entered service in September 1961 and would be withdrawn by WMPTE in January 1974. It is working on the 8 route to Rawnsley via Hednesford. (R. F. Mack)

900 (900 MDH)

Below: After a long association with Willowbrook, the Loughborough coachbuilder, which had begun in 1953 when trolleybus 850 (RDH 990) was delivered that September, it all came to an end exactly eleven years later when 900 (900 MDH) arrived. The order for ten 30-foot-long AEC Regent V 2D2RAs with consecutive chassis numbers was split equally between Metro-Cammell and Willowbrook, with the latter bodying the last five. On a warm sunny day, 900 is loading up with passengers in St Paul's Bus Station before leaving on a 6 route shortworking to the Elms Hotel in Aldridge. (P. J. Relf)

61 (761 UDH)

Above: The last front-engined buses bought by Walsall Corporation was a surprising order for fifteen forward-entrance Daimler CVG6s with H37/28F bodies built by Metro-Cammell. They arrived in the spring of 1963 and were painted in the light blue livery with three thin chrome yellow bands. 61 (61 UDH), the first of the class, is parked near to St Paul's Bus Station in about 1965. These buses were built with thicker upper saloon body frames, which was a typical MCCW/Weymann body feature and was done in order to brace the body in the area of the staircase and the front bulkhead. (Photobus)

62 (762 UDH)

Left: About to leave Heath Hayes on the 47 service from Walsall to Cannock in June 1964 is 62 (762 UDH) when it was only fifteen months old. This Daimler CVG6 had a useful seating capacity of sixty-five with a 27-foot length but was the last of its breed as far as front-engined buses were concerned as after these all future purchases, with one notable exception, were short-length rear-engined Daimler Fleetlines. This bus was taken out of service by June 1975, when operated by West Midlands PTE. (D. F. Parker)

66 (766 UDH)

Above: The centre of Dudley is very hilly, and during the many years that the bus station was located in Birmingham there were a number of bad accidents when buses rolled away. The driver of this 1963 Daimler CVG6 has been very wise and has chocked his vehicle, which is parked alongside the late 1960s Churchill Precinct. 66 (766 UDH), with its forward-entrance MCCW H37/28F body, is looking a little shabby in its West Midlands PTE livery and is working on the 265 service to Walsall, though in earlier years when this service was the 65 it went via Walsall to Stafford. (D. R. Harvey Collection)

71 (771 UDH)

Below: Daimler 71 (771 UDH), a Metro-Cammell-bodied Daimler CVG6, has turned from Paradise Street into Queen Street and is approaching the West Bromwich terminus when working on the 14 service. The bus had entered service in May 1963 and was one the first to be withdrawn in June 1975, but outlived a few of the Edgley Cox specification short-length Daimler Fleetlines. The whole of this central area of West Bromwich has now been extensively redeveloped and is part of the pedestrianised High Street scheme. (A. Yates)

75 (775 UDH)

Leaving the row of bus stops in St Paul's Street is 75 (775 UDH) when working on the 41 service to Willenhall via New Invention. The unusual feature of these Metro-Cammell-bodied Daimler CVG6 was their white rubber-mounted windows. 75 arrived in Walsall in May 1963 and they were used on the same types of services that the 30-foot-long, forward-entrance, front-engined buses of 1961. Unfortunately, the bodywork of these buses was yet again somewhat basic and they reverberated and rattled their way around Walsall until, in the case of 75, it was withdrawn in February 1977. (R. H. G. Simpson)

11

The Fleetline Era

Throughout the early 1960s, the need for new motorbuses in Walsall was becoming pressing, but trolleybus routes were expanded to new estates north of Bloxwich and second-hand trolleybuses were purchased from Maidstone & District, Ipswich and Grimsby-Cleethorpes. This situation continued until the joint trolleybus service with Wolverhampton Corporation had to be abandoned because of the construction of the M6 motorway, which crossed the route at Bentley. This closure occurred on 31 October 1965. The trolleybus system began its terminal decline on 10 March 1968 when the Sunday operation of trolleybuses ended. As late as 1969 a Parliamentary Bill was sought for the construction of five further trolleybus route extensions, and had not the PTE taken over, almost all of the surviving Bournemouth Corporation Sunbeam MF2B two-door trolleybuses were to be purchased. The Corporation was, right up to the last months of its independence, an enthusiastic proponent of trolleybuses. The Walsall trolleybus system, despite being a successful operation, had become something of an anachronism, and due to the lack of spare parts, new trolleybus manufacturers and the general lack of national enthusiasm for trolleybuses, the Walsall system was therefore an early target for replacement by its new owners. The last routes were all closed on 2 October 1970 by West Midlands PTE.

By the early 1960s, it was becoming obvious that trolleybus manufacturing was coming to a close and that many of the motorbus fleet were approaching withdrawal. In collaboration with Transport Vehicles (Daimler) Limited, the General Manager designed an ultra-short-length centre-entrance Daimler Fleetline CRG6LX, which was exhibited at the 1962 Commercial Motor Show. Although of short length at 25 ft 7½ in., it nevertheless seated sixty-four passengers and was designed to gain access to any area in Walsall, especially those on housing estates where roads were narrow and turns were tight. The design was modified to 27 ft 6 in., becoming the basis for a fleet of similar Northern Counties-bodied Fleetlines, delivered between 1963 and 1965. The 1965 batch were also to this length and had a new dual-door design of Northern Counties body. The last forty-eight Fleetlines were again slightly longer at 28 ft 6 in. and were seventy-seaters but had a small door opposite the driver for one-man operation while retaining the large central door. They were delivered as Walsall's last motorbuses by February 1969, with 119 (XDH 519G) being numerically the final Walsall bus the final Walsall bus. Mr R. Edgley Cox had proposed as late as 1967 a 35-foot-long three-door, two-axle double-decker trolleybus, but this was rejected. It reappeared, albeit in a much modified form, as the one-off 36-foot-long Daimler Fleetline 50 (XDH 56G).

1 (1 UDH)

Above: An official Northern Counties photograph of 1 (1 UDH), the first short-length Daimler Fleetline CRG6LX, in November 1962, around the time of it being exhibited at the 1962 Commercial Motor Show, reveals just how much of a radical departure it was. The idea behind the reduced length of these buses was to try to get high capacity buses into areas where entry was awkward, such as roads in housing estates, thereby enabling more people access to a bus service. The first noticeable feature was that it had no front overhang and the entrance to the cab was through an opening in the centre of the front bulkhead. The bus was only 25 feet 7½ inches long but still managed to have a seating capacity of sixty-four. The bus had the Gardner 6LX 10.45 litre engine, unlike the subsequent batches, numbered 2–30, that had the smaller 6LW engine. (NCME)

1 (1 UDH)

Below: 1 (1 UDH) was perhaps the most significant bus bought during Mr Edgley Cox's tenure as General Manager of Walsall Corporation since the first trailblazing 30-foot-long Sunbeam F4A trolleybus of 1955. This had entered service in November of that year and was the prototype short-length Daimler Fleetline CRG6LX and had a Northern Counties centre-entrance body. With experience of operation, it proved to be too short and cramped at 25 feet 7½ inches, but was still a revolutionary vehicle and paved the way for ninety-eight further buses, albeit built to a slightly longer specification. It is travelling into Walsall along Hatherton Road having worked on the 5 route from Hednesford. (D. R. Harvey Collection)

1 (1 UDH)

Above: Standing in the bus parking area in St Paul's Street in about 1972 is 1 (1 UDH), by now numbered 1L. It has been repainted in the West Midlands PTE livery, which emphasises the ungainliness of the front end, which looks as if it has been stuck onto the rear of a standard NCME body. Despite it being such a one-off prototype, 1 UDH was withdrawn after a surprisingly long time in service, in August 1974, and even then it languished for almost three years in Birchills Garage while several abortive proposals were made to keep this unique bus. Alas nothing happened! (D. R. Harvey Collection)

3 (2733 DH)

Below: The more squared-up front end of 3 (2733 DH) is evident as it waits in Walsall Road at The Bull Stake in Darlaston. The front overhang on this batch of buses was reduced and the vehicles had an increased length of 27 feet 6 inches, while the driving position was moved forward to a position slightly in front of the front axle. Despite their short length, the seating capacity of the Northern Counties body was increased to H41/29F configuration, which at best was cosy and at worst extremely cramped. The deliveries of these Northern Counties seventy-seaters up to the E-registered ones of 1967 all had Gardner 6LW 8.4 litre engines, but 3, unlike all but two others of the 1964 batch of single-door vehicles, remained a single-door bus and was withdrawn in December 1970. (Roy Marshall)

8 (2738 DH)

Above: Short-length Daimler Fleetline CRG6LW 8 (2738 DH) was fitted with a Perkins V8 510 8,840cc engine in April 1967, which was subsequently replaced by the Phase 2 model in July 1968, although the rear panels did not display the Perkins interlocking four ring badge. By now carrying WM fablon stickers, the bus is otherwise in as built condition and is getting well loaded up as it stands outside Boots the Chemists in Walsall town centre. It was to revert to a standard Gardner 6LW engine during its operational life with West Midlands PTE. (D. R. Harvey Collection)

10 (2740 DH)

Below: On leaving Aldridge, the 6 service returned to Walsall by way of Walsall Road. This is now the A454. The industrial works behind the bus has now been swamped by new housing developments, although the farmland at Berryfields Farm survives. Walsall's Daimler Fleetline CRG6LW 10 (2740 DH) was one of the original production batch of 27 ft 6 in. short-length Northern Counties H44/29F buses delivered in February 1964. With their driving position over the front axle, they were very pleasant to ride in as they held the road extremely well. Their centre entrance and sliding door were not designed for One-Man-Operation. After acquisition by WMPTE on 1 October 1969, nearly all were converted to a dual-door layout, which placed a single-leaf door opposite the driver. This conversion work was undertaken by Lex Garages of Stourbridge, and although successful it was aesthetically quite awful. The job was turned down by Northern Counties, the original body-builder, while Willowbrook's tender failed to win the contract. The bus is speeding past Longwood Lane and is being followed by a 'lowline' Ford Consul 204E that was in production from February 1959 until 1962. (D. R. Harvey Collection)

11 (2741 DH)

Above: Just pulling out of Walsall Bus Station is 11 (2741 DH). This bus had entered service in February 1964 and is still relatively new as it begins its journey on the 12 route to Pelsall. The curved windscreen and upper saloon front windows were developed by Northern Counties from bodies mounted on front-entrance chassis built for Barton Transport of Chilwell on Dennis Loline and AEC Regent V chassis. 11 was rebuilt to a dual-door bus by Lex Garages in October 1972 and remained in this condition until withdrawn exactly four years later. (L. Mason)

15 (2745 DH)

Below: Travelling into Wolverhampton on 22 March 1973 in full West Midlands livery is Northern Counties Daimler Fleetline CRG6LW 15 (2745 DH). It is turning out of Park Lane when working on the WMPTE 98 route. Rebuilt with effectively a new front end fitted to the existing upper saloon, the combination of upper saloon curves and a square lower saloon frontage was not a happy one. The seating capacity after the rebuilding by Lex Garages remained at seventy but the narrow single-leaf front door was impractical for loading, adding to the normal slowness of loading an OMO bus. The sign in the nearside front window between the doors directs passengers to the front entrance and indicates that the large sliding door is the exit. (E. V. Trigg)

17 (2747 DH)

Above: On 25 February 1967, the original Northern Counties body of Daimler Fleetline CRG6LW 17 (2747 DH) was virtually destroyed by fire and was rebodied by the same coachbuilders with the contemporary body style with the later style of window pans. It re-entered service in May 1968. As a result of this rebodying, it was not rebuilt as it was already of the final type of H41/29D layout with a two-door layout. It is unloading its passengers on a very wet day after working on the 59 service in full WMPTE livery. (D. R. Harvey Collection)

19 (ADH 119B)

Below: Standing in the outside demonstration park at Earl's Court for the 1964 Commercial Motor Show is 19 (ADH 119B). As a result of this appearance, the bus entered service slightly later in October 1964. The bus was finished to exhibition standards with extra chrome fittings. It was one of the stars of that year's show but the body style on the shortened wheelbase only prompted one other order, being from the SHM&DJB. 19 displayed the basic flaw in Mr Edgley Cox's design, in that without major alterations it was converted it could never be operated as an OMO vehicle, for which in January 1972 it was converted. (D. Akrigg)

27 (BDH 427C)

Above: Turning left into Bull Street from Priory Queensway in West Midlands PTE livery as the renumbered 27L, the true horror of the rebuilding of these already idiosyncratically styled Northern Counties bodies can be appreciated. It was soon evident to their new owners that the former Walsall buses could be rebuilt to accommodate a single-leaf front door, thereby utilising the wasted space of the original design alongside the driver and enabling the bus to be converted to one-man operation. The result was an extremely practical solution, but the end product did not win many prizes in the good looks stakes, especially as these were the last of the type to retain the curved upper saloon front windows! 27 (BDH 427C) was rebuilt and re-entered service in February 1972 and ran in this condition before being withdrawn just over five years later. (D. R. Harvey Collection)

30 (BDH 430C)

Below: Parked near the Corporation's mobile tea bar in Bradford Place is 30 (BDH 430C). This was the only one of the originally front-entrance Northern Counties-bodied Daimler Fleetline CRG6LWs to have this style of flat front. It was the last of the single-entrance short-length Fleetlines from the batch of six buses that entered service in January 1965 and, as well as its unique flat front end, it had a standard set of NCME front windows. The result was not a happy compromise and the bus was subsequently rebuilt by Lex Garages with a standard narrow front entrance in April 1972. It was finally withdrawn by WMPTE in October 1976. (D. R. Harvey Collection)

34 (EDH 634C)

Above: In 1962 Mr R. Edgley Cox instigated the design of a 25 ft 7 in. long Daimler Fleetline, which became numbered 1 in the Walsall fleet. The aim was to provide a more manoeuvrable rear-engined double-decker and this was achieved by shortening the front overhang and effectively placing the driver over the front axle. However, 1 UDH was just too cramped and in 1963 the first production short-length Fleetlines, by now stretched by nearly 2 feet, were placed into service. Despite their short length, the Northern Counties bodies managed to accommodate some seventy passengers. Between October 1963 and February 1969 ninety-nine of these strange-looking buses entered service and could therefore claim to be the only standardised double-decker in Walsall's fleet! In pristine condition, 34 (EDH 634C) is parked on the waste ground opposite the Transport offices in St Paul's Street when new in 1965. Parked next to it is 880 (880 HDH), one of the Willowbrook-bodied Dennis Loline Mark IIs, purchased in 1960. On the right is 960 SDH, a Ford Thames 15 cwt Dormobile minibus that was used by the Transport Department for staff transport. (J. Cockshot)

41 (EDH 941C)

Below: Leaving the bus shelters in High Street, Bloxwich, is 41 (EDH 941C), a Daimler Fleetline CRG6LW. This Northern Counties H41/29D-bodied bus entered service in October 1965 and is working on the long 1 route from Hednesford via Cannock and Great Wyrley, with the conductor standing on the front platform in the days before OMO. Behind the bus is the mock-Tudor Mitchell & Butler's-owned Bull's Head Public House, and parked in Park Road is a three-year-old 1964 Walsall-registered hard-top Sunbeam Alpine Mark IV sports car, which was spoilt by its ability to rust at an alarming rate. (D. R. Harvey Collection)

53 (EDH 953C)

Above: Turning into St Paul's Street from Hatherton Road as it approaches the bus station is 53 (EDH 953C). The bus is another of the Gardner 6LW-engined Daimler Fleetlines with a Northern Counties H41/29D body and is working on the 23 service to Walsall Wood, Brownhills and Ogley Hay. These buses were slightly longer at 28 ft 6 in. long, and with the more conventional upper saloon front windows, they were not so unbalanced looking as the earlier short-length Fleetlines. 53 was to pass into the ownership of West Midlands PTE and lasted in service until January 1978. (D. R. Harvey Collection)

56 (XDH 56C)

Below: 56 (XDH 56G) was the solitary Daimler Fleetline CRC6-36 to be supplied to a British operator as all of the other sixteen went to Johannesburg in South Africa. The chassis was fitted with a Cummins V6-200 9.63 litre engine and an automatic gearbox and was sent to Northern Counties in June 1968, and was subsequently exhibited at the 1968 Commercial Motor Show at Earl's Court. It was fitted with a H51/35D body but was re-seated to H51/34D in April 1969. This bus was the only tangible outcome to Mr Edgley Cox's proposal for a 35-foot-long, two-axle OMO double-decker trolleybus with three doors and two staircases, which never got beyond the drawing board. Not long after it entered service, 56 is in St Paul's Bus Station on 15 April 1969 when working on the prestigious 118 service to Birmingham via the Scott Arms in Great Barr. The troublesome Cummins engine was never very reliable and as a result the bus spent a lot of its short working life of just over five years off the road under repair in Birchills Garage. (A. J. Douglas)

56 (XDH 56C)

Above: The sheer length of the behemoth that was 56 is noticeable in this nearside official Northern Counties photograph, taken in Wigan before it travelled south for the 1968 Commercial Show at Earl's Court. This was the final surprise of the managership of Mr Edgley Cox, who in one fell swoop went from the shortest of all Daimler Fleetlines to the longest! This 35 ft 9 in. long double-deck bus was based on the CRC6-36 chassis originally designed to meet a specification for Johannesburg Municipal Transport in South Africa. The body design incorporated a front entrance and rear exit, each with its own staircase, and accommodated eighty-six passengers, with fifty-one on the top deck, and numerous special features such as a closed-circuit television monitor to allow driver supervision of the rear door. The Achilles heel of the bus was to be found at the rear, wherein lay the noisy, rough-running Cummins V6-200 engine, which had also been fitted to the ill-fated Daimler Roadliner SRC6, and it was that that all but condemned 56 to joining the category of the unloved. (NCME)

56 (XDH 56C)

Below: Parked at the Buses Festival at the Rover Heritage Museum at Gaydon on 21 August 2016 is the preserved 56 (XDH 56C). The bus was completed on 3 December 1968, the livery being in a more subdued blue-grey than Walsall's usual shade of blue. The length was emphasised by the low overall height of 13 ft 10 in. On 1 October 1969 it passed with the remainder of the Walsall undertaking to the newly formed West Midlands PTE, remaining in original livery, and was used only intermittently before being withdrawn in May 1974. After this, the bus went through the hands of various independents before being sold for preservation and beautifully restored at the Wythall Bus Museum. (D. R. Harvey)

79 (KDH 897E)

Above: Leaving the bus station in St Paul's Street is Daimler Fleetline CRG6LW 79 (KDH 897E), working on the former trolleybus route 32 to Lower Farm to the north-east of Bloxwich. These buses had a standard Fleetline 16 ft 3 in. wheelbase and the NCME H41/29D body was 28 ft 6 in. long. Towering behind the bus is the large nave of St Paul's Church, built in 1893 in the Decorated style and noticeable for lacking a tower. 79 is in the pale blue Corporation livery with three thin chrome yellow livery stripes in which it was delivered in January 1967. (D. R. Harvey Collection)

81 (KDH 881E)

Below: Travelling into Railway Street with the former Chubb Lock building factory behind it is 81 (KDH 881E). This Daimler Fleetline CRG6LW is working on the 9 route to the former Wolverhampton Corporation trolleybus terminus at Jeffcock Road. The bus is in the full Walsall Corporation livery but, as the WM fablon stickers reveal, it is now owned by West Midlands PTE. The notice in the front side window informs intending passengers to board through the narrow front door. The bus is being followed by a Farina-styled Morris Oxford V, a Honda C50 moped, an Austin 1100, a Morris Minor 1000 Traveller and a rear-engined Hillman Imp. (L. Mason)

93 (KDH 93F)

Above: Cresting the hump-backed bridge over the Birmingham & Fazeley Canal in Lancaster Street is 93 (KDH 93F). This was the third member of the 1968 batch of Daimler Fleetlines, all of which were fitted with the larger Gardner 10.45 litre 6LX engine and had NCME H41/29D bodywork. From this angle it is apparent that the deep 'V'-shaped windscreen does not fit well with the flat front of the upper saloon. The bus is working on the 258 service from Walsall, quite soon after it had been taken into the West Midlands PTE fleet on 1 October 1969, but in true Walsall Corporation style it is wearing an advertisement for the locally brewed Highgate Mild beer. (J. Carroll)

98 (RDH 98F)

Below: The Birmingham city centre terminus of the 158 service was at the Corporation Street end of Union Street, alongside the then derelict City Arcade. Union Street had replaced Martineau Street on 16 October 1960 as the terminus for a number of Birmingham bus services, including the 33 service to Kingstanding, so for reasons of continuity it was used for the Walsall Corporation service, which began on 21 June 1965. Walsall's 98 (RDH 98F), a short-length Daimler Fleetline CRG6LX with a Northern Counties H41/29D body, dating from February 1968, stands outside the City Arcade in Union Street in early 1969. The driver and conductor are both standing on the front platform, which would soon be history as 98 would be converted to OMO in February 1971. (L. Mason)

107 (XDH 507G)

Above: Leaving the stygian gloom of the Birmingham Bus Station beneath the Bull Ring Centre is 107 (XDH 507G). It is working back to Walsall by way of Walsall Road and the Scott Arms at Great Barr. Entering service in January 1969, it would only operate in this condition for nine months before the Walsall municipal crests would disappear under the fablon WM fleetname stickers. The last batch of fourteen G-suffix registered short-length Daimler Fleetlines had a reduced lower saloon seating capacity, making their layout H41/27D. (L. Mason)

108 (XDH 508G)

Below: A number of the short-length Daimler Fleetlines were painted with yellow front panels. This was to make them more visible, especially when manoeuvring in bus stations. Appropriately enough, 108 (XDH 508G) is parked outside the offices at the top end of St Paul's Bus Station and has been working on the short circular 24 service to Chuckery and Paddock. 108 had been one of the first four of the XDH G-suffix registration buses to enter service in December 1968 but spent most of its life operating as an OMO bus for West Midlands PTE, not being withdrawn until April 1980, after which it was swiftly despatched to Booths of Rotherham for scrapping. (L. Mason)

113 (XDH 513G)

Above: Loading up with passengers in Queen Street in Wolverhampton when working on the 30 service is 113 (XDH 513G). It was operating for West Midlands PTE but has not yet been renumbered to 113L. The bus had been recently equipped for one-man operation in August 1970. The former Wolverhampton Corporation bus stop clearly states that this is the stop for Rough Hills, yet the destination blind has misspelt the name of the destination. According to Nikolaus Pevsner, Queen Street is the best street in Wolverhampton and 113 is parked outside the row of Regency properties on the south side of the street. (L. Mason)

116 (XDH 516G)

Below: About to turn from Dudley Street into Edgbaston Street in the early summer of 1969 is 116 (XDH 516G). It is leaving Birmingham city centre on the former Midland Red 118 service back to Walsall via the Scott Arms Public House. 116 was among the last five new buses to enter service with Walsall Corporation, in February 1969. 116 became the very last short-length Northern Counties-bodied Daimler Fleetline CRG6LX to be withdrawn, this occurring in May 1985, although the PTE continued to operate it in a restored condition until April 1986. It was subsequently sold for preservation and is housed at the Bus Museum at Wythall. (R. F. Mack)

2888 (C888 FON)

Above: West Midlands Travel beautifully repainted a number of MCW Metrobus II 102/64s with MCW H43/30F bodies in the former constituent municipal liveries of Birmingham, Coventry, Walsall, West Bromwich and Wolverhampton Corporations. These buses were repainted with a fine attention to detail and original municipal crests and legal lettering. In the centre, next to the author's 2489 (JOJ 489), a former Birmingham City Transport Crossley-bodied Crossley DD42/6 dating from July 1950, is 3030 (F30 XOF) in the reproduced Birmingham livery. On the extreme left is the Mark II Metrobus 2888 (C888 FON), in the livery of Walsall Corporation. They are all at the transport open day at the Black Country Living Museum on 6 June 1996 and for quite a few years these heritage repaints were to be found at local events, historical galas and transport rallies such as this one. (D. R. Harvey)

2888 (C888 FON)

Below: Travelling down St Paul's Street opposite the bus station is 2888 (C888 FON), the MCW Metrobus II DR102/48 with a MCW H43/30F body. On 21 July 1997 it is working on the 341 service from Willenhall via New Invention, which had formerly been Walsall's 41 route. New in August 1985, the bus was chosen as one of the buses to be repainted in the heritage municipal liveries and was very accurately repainted in Walsall Corporation's light blue with thin chrome yellow bands. This bus was the last one ever to receive the Walsall livery and it is appropriate to end this look at the Walsall bus fleet with 2888 reminding the townsfolk of what their bus fleet used to look like. (D. R. Harvey)

Bibliography

The main source of statistical information comes from the PSV Circle fleet history 2PD6 (2005), *Walsall Corporation*, and my own *A Nostalgic Tour of Walsall by Tram, Trolleybus and Bus*, published by Silver Link in 1999, *Dennis Buses* by Robin Hannay, published by Ian Allan, and an unpublished work, *Walsall Memories*, by Jack Haddock. Further local history books that were most useful were *Around The Town*, published by Walsall Local History Centre (1991); *Walsall Past and Present* by David Vodden (1999); *Walsall Revisited* by David Vodden (1997); and *Bloxwich* by David Vodden (1997), all published by Alan Sutton Publishing. In addition, *The Black Country* by Harold Parsons, published by Robert Hale, and *The Buildings of England – Staffordshire* by Nikolaus Pevsner, published by Penguin in 1975, provided valuable information. Minutes and press cuttings assembled by myself during my long association as Hon. Secretary for the Birmingham Transport Historical Group were a valuable source of information, as were researches in both the Dudley archives, then in Coseley, and the Walsall archives in Essex Street. Additional information was obtained in the archives of Walsall Reference Library and Birmingham Central Reference Library.

Acknowledgements

The author is grateful to the many photographers acknowledged in the text who have contributed to this volume. I sincerely thank all of those who are still alive for allowing me to use pictures, many of which were taken more than sixty years ago. Thanks are also especially due to Alan Broughall, the late Les Mason, the late Bob Mills and the late Ray Wilson, who all allowed me to print all their photographs many years ago and generously gave permission for me to use their material. Where the photographer is not known, the photographs are credited to my own collection. Special thanks are due to my wife Diana for her usual advice and splendid proof reading.

The book would not have been possible without the continued encouragement given by Connor Stait and Louis Archard at Amberley Publishing.